Series Contents

What is Wellness?

Free Will and Language

The Enemy

I Am Physical

I Am Spiritual

I Am Intellectual

I Am Emotional

I Am Occupational

I Am Social

I Am Environmental

The End of the Age
(End Time Prophesy Analysis)

Doing All to Stand
(End Time Survival Strategy for Abundant Life)

I AM WELL

Greg,
Stay well
and
be blessed!

I Am Well, Part One: What is Wellness?

By Jonathan Moore

First Edition | Copyright © 2023 by I Am Well Ministries

ISBN 978-1-66788-303-8 (Print)

ISBN 978-1-66788-304-5 (eBook)

I Am Well Ministries
www.iamwellministries.org

All Scripture quotations in this book are from the King James Version of the Bible, unless otherwise indicated.

Disclaimer:
The information presented in this book is the author's opinion and does not constitute medical, legal, psychological, psychiatric, or financial advice. Reader agrees that author and/or publisher will not be held liable for any damages, real or perceived that arise from reader's implementation of any topic discussed in this book. Reader agrees to take full responsibility for their own choices and actions in life, holding author and/or publisher completely blameless and harmless in perpetuity.

Part One Contents

Preface

Those desiring a mature understanding of wellness can indeed embark upon a lifetime adventure of seeking, implementing, evaluating and refining. This creates a cycle of re-implementing, re-evaluating, re-refining, and several different types of death and rebirth along the way. This adventure requires honing, balancing, disciplining, and humbling processes. Our understanding of most aspects of life is limited. Since we serve a limitless God who has neither a beginning nor an end, and He is the author, only He has a perfect understanding of wellness. I've been intentionally pursuing wellness, as I will define it in this book, for over 20 years. For over ten years now I have known that I was called to write this book. I believe there is wisdom found in embracing a strategy of waiting to accumulate a formidable depth of experience before attempting to articulate such a profound and meaningful topic, hence my hesitancy to put "pen-to-paper". I've also struggled tremendously to implement a life of wellness. The struggle has been so intense, that it has felt like a roller coaster of successes and failures. How can I teach on a subject that I haven't quite mastered? I felt like a hypocrite to preach about wellness when my own personal life has sometimes been terribly out of balance. But I've come to the realization that the struggles and battles are a necessary part of the conversation. It turns out you can't actually have true wellness without them! The Lord in His goodness has allowed intense and diverse tribulations in my life, and given me the strength to overcome, I believe specifically so that I would carry forth this wellness message, a message based on a life that consists of tragedies and invitations to overcome, a life that is full of different roads, a plethora of choices, opportunities to improve and balance, and the gift of a life worth living, full of excitement, danger, drama, and glory. Whether or not a person can verbally define wellness, the degree of wellness implementation they accomplish directly correlates to the quality of their life, and the legacy they will leave. Our understanding of wellness is only a reality in the briefest of moments, a snap-shot in time, and while truth is constant and never changing, our understanding changes as we continue to seek and more pieces of the puzzle are brought into perspective. I know that the Lord has called me to use this present moment to share what I currently understand to be true regarding wellness. Hopefully my understanding will continue to improve and mature over time. I know though, that the present understanding with which the Lord has gifted me is more than sufficient to be a tremendous blessing to many, and could have eternal consequences for some. I believe the Lord will use the message contained herein to break off demonic chains of oppression, ignorance, deception, hatred and control, so that His children can be free to live powerfully, courageously, faithfully, wisely, and to live joyfully and victoriously with peace in their hearts. I believe strongly that if you take the time to really focus, process, and implement what I will share, you will become a mighty and powerful warrior and servant of the one true God, the Lord Jesus Christ of Nazareth, such that the gates of hell will not prevail against you. I trust that those among us who are able to more fully grasp the true concept of wellness have a strong likelihood of living an abundantly full life, and will indeed stand strong against everything and anything the devil will throw at them in the coming end of days. This is not a book about how to be wealthy and strong and successful, *(although I believe the principles contained herein definitely lend themselves to those possibilities being likely to manifest in your life),* but rather, this book is about truly becoming the person God created you to be, completing His assignments with excellence, and one day hearing those precious and coveted words, "Well done, good and faithful servant". It's about courageously, wisely, and vigorously completing the race and winning the true prize, life everlasting with our Heavenly Father. Welcome to the wellness conversation! Just be aware that by reading this book, you're moving higher up the enemy's hit list. Prepare yourself for increased joy and favor, but also... prepare yourself for battle.

The thief cometh not, but for to steal, and to kill, and to destroy:

I am come that they might have life, and that they might have it more abundantly.

John 10:10

Introduction

Much of what I share in this book is valuable to both Christians and non-Christians. Truth is truth, and what works, works, so implementation of the ideas presented will result in order, function, and health, all things that tend to produce a more thoroughly enjoyable life. There are some truths that will be shared here, however, that will not be received by non-Christians and, therefore, they will not immediately perceive those pieces of information as beneficial to them. I encourage everyone who finds this book in their hand to fully engage with it regardless of where your faith stands. Study it. Challenge it. Implement the parts in which you readily perceive value, and at least consider, if only briefly, the parts with which you take offense or disagree. No matter what your current faith status, there will be much shared of great value for your life, and the lives of those you love.

Any decent attempt to thoroughly cover a topic like wellness will require a lengthy discussion to say the least. The more you gain an understanding of what wellness is truly, the more you will begin to see how literally everything in life is connected in seemingly countless ways. This means that the vast expanse of knowledge offered in every single book ever written has some implication and pertinence to the topic of wellness. This presents a risk that the conversation could become too long and impractical, and therefore of none-effect or limited benefit to the reader if we focus on any specific topic for too long. I will do my best to provide a balance between being thorough and concise. I will attempt to explain the definition of wellness, how one goes about understanding, developing, and implementing a life of wellness, the meaning and impacts derived therefrom, and how I see wellness as it relates to biblical end time prophesy.

I was in the fitness industry for over 20 years and one of the questions I always asked people when interviewing them for a job at a gym was, "What is the difference between fitness and wellness?" Overwhelmingly the answers showed a lack of understanding. Usually I got responses like, "Well, fitness is about being strong and fast, and wellness is about being healthy". Some applicants with greater knowledge of fitness like a certified personal trainer usually had some decent understanding of fitness, but there was always a kind of blank stare when it came to describing how wellness was different.

There are some people out there who discuss wellness in fantastic detail, but what I have seen is the vast majority of those voices are speaking from a New-Age religion perspective. This is very dangerous because people recognize some truth being shared, and then open themselves up to everything the misled teacher has to say. Then, many become led astray and deceived by false doctrine. They are literally swallowing poison in the form of lies that are creating death, destruction, and potentially eternal damnation. I'm going to do my best here to break down wellness from a true Christian perspective, so people are getting the truth, the whole truth, and nothing but the truth! It's a shame really that so many of the people in the wellness community are wise in some areas, and yet deceived in the ones that matter most. It's also quite sad and unfortunate that the information I'm going to share is not widely taught from the pulpit. Most of our churches today are not even preaching the full gospel, much less speaking to any of these other topics. We are beautifully complex, created in the image of God, and the holy temple that is our body deserves our attention. We should learn how to care for and operate the vessel with which God has trusted us. We should strive to understand the significance of the miracle that we are indeed spirit, soul, and body. A great understanding of how our spirit, soul, and body interact will produce a most useful servant whom God can use to bring His name glory. A poor understanding of these invaluable interactions will produce a servant who is not finely tuned for job performance. I see parallel illustration in the parable of the talents. (*Yes, I know a "talent" was a unit of weight used in commerce, often to measure money. I believe the parable reveals truth about our management of the financial resources we are trusted to steward, as well as every other gift we have that can be leveraged to serve others.*) We are on our way to becoming "good and faithful servants" when we are faithful to manage our talent (spirit, soul, and body) well, and the inverse is obviously true; a failure to focus an adequate amount of energy toward understanding how who-we-are works, sets those slothful servants on course for outer darkness, and weeping and gnashing of teeth. Am I being dramatic? I really don't think so. In fact, the importance has still been understated, but I hope to articulate significance over the course of this book so that a fire will be ignited within you to become that servant who uses every talent the Lord has given you. I hope to also empower you with the tools to become that person. To do so, first we must frame the conversation with some context.

"Man, just what is this wellness thing this guy is so worked up over?"

Chapter 1: What is Wellness?

I mentioned in the introduction section that when interviewing someone for a gym related position I always asked them, "What is the difference between fitness and wellness?" The responses were always pitifully inadequate, if not completely wrong, even from people with Bachelor's and Master's Degrees in Exercise Science! Why is this, and how could it be? I'll go into that later, but first let me answer my own question and give us our initial definition of wellness from which to build upon. When asked about wellness, most people lean toward their understanding of physical fitness. It's helpful, then, to begin the conversation by asking, "What is the difference between fitness and wellness?"

Fitness is generally accepted as being measured by five components:
- Muscular Strength
- Muscular Endurance
- Cardiovascular Endurance
- Flexibility
- Body Composition

These are all areas that a personal trainer or health coach can assess, measure, set goals upon, and improve. For example, if someone is really strong and has a great ability to recover from stress, but can't touch their toes, then we can prescribe a stretching routine that will help to focus improvement to the area where they are lacking. The standards for how to measure each component and determine whether a person assesses as poor or excellent in each area have come from highly respected academic and professional institutions (mainly universities) through scientific research and experience over time. I will go into greater detail on the components of fitness later, but for now an intro to them is helpful in distinguishing *(or clarifying through setting apart by pointing out differences)* between fitness and wellness. When most people hear words like "health" or "wellness", their understanding leans toward some definition of physical fitness. The truth is it's so much more! I first began hearing more detailed conversations about wellness when I was in college, working at the school's gym. The university had a group called the University Wellness Council. I was not on this council, but I and the fitness staff worked with them on several different campus projects over the years, and I was friends with people on the council. The work they did more than caught my attention, it changed the course of my life. They defined wellness as being made up of seven components.

The seven components of wellness are generally accepted as being:
- Physical
- Spiritual
- Intellectual
- Emotional
- Occupational
- Social
- Environmental

As with fitness, it is possible to assess, measure, set goals upon, and improve each of these areas of wellness. So, someone could be in pretty awesome shape physically, they could be really smart and really balanced emotionally, but if they don't have a job or any friends, then they are suffering in those components/ areas and the theory is that bringing remedy to the lacking areas will result in a person who is more balanced, therefore happier and healthier, and someone who will live longer. Give that person a job and some friends and they are better off right? Perhaps! But not always necessarily. You have to qualify the remedy. What if the new friends end up stealing from them or causing them to get arrested? What if the physical fitness that was previously so excellent is harmed by the new job which causes them to lose sleep, go long periods of time without eating, and subjects them to an abusive boss and dangerous working conditions? Once you take a moment to reflect on the seven components of wellness you can quickly begin to see how all of the areas impact each other in an endlessly complex set of matrixes. Usually, all seven components affect each other simultaneously, with most actions and choices affecting some areas disproportionately. We find it possible then to make a choice which improves one or several areas, but that takes away from or harms some of the other areas. Life for most people becomes reactionary; once a wellness component becomes harmed severely, it gets attention at the detriment of other components, until another area's suffering becomes the squeaky wheel and it gets attention. Most people unfortunately go through life trying to repair what is damaged, rather than fine tuning and tweaking all of the areas wisely so that they can stay ahead of the curve and make progress toward all areas improving proactively. Proactively managing your wellness requires diligent effort, but it is possible and sure beats the alternative!

The more we understand the collective impact that our choices have on all of the different areas, we begin to develop a greater appreciation for the symphony that is wellness. We are the conductor, doing our best to get all of the different instruments to play the right notes, in the right order, at the right time, at the optimal volume to create music. Whether we are aware of this job or not, we are all orchestra conductors. Some of us make beautiful music, some of us make terrible music, and some others can barely seem to produce a single note. Some are able to manage the complexities of life long enough to produce a few measures of good music, while others are able to create volumes of scores throughout their lifetime that inspire and encourage generations. These are the wellness savants. Those who understand who they are, what they are working with, how what they are working with interacts with the world around them, who they were created to be, and how to fully leverage their talents with constrained time and limited resources. I believe we should all strive to make as much beautiful "music" as possible with the time we have.

When we become better at balancing and optimizing wellness personally, our lives usually become overwhelmingly healthier, more productive, and more meaningful. The more a family unit can appropriately balance each member's wellness, the better the family unit is overall. Obviously, this idea continues to carry further and further as we look at larger and larger groups of people. From small businesses to entire industries, communities, cities, states, countries, continents and ultimately the entire world, the more individuals are optimizing their lives through careful and diligent maintenance of each area of wellness personally, the healthier and more productive the group will be. The really cool part is that each additional person who gets it right produces an increasing return. So, the more people get their stuff together personally, obviously the better things are for everyone, but the return is exponential as the synergy between two optimally well persons or groups produces greater than a 1:1 return. In the similar way that two people lending a hand can cut the time to complete a task (it might take 1 person an hour to complete a task, but 2 people can get it done in 15 minutes, not 30), each additional person living a life of wellness becomes a multiplier for others they interact with in life. Unfortunately, similarly, a person who is terribly out of balance and dysfunctional is usually a multiplier of chaos and destruction in the lives of the people around them. The implication of the responsibility we have not just to ourselves, but also to our families and communities becomes painfully clearer the greater we understand how we are all connected and dependent on each other. It's a terrible burden and responsibility to which most are ignorant. Some people self-sabotage, usually not understanding that their efforts to be selfish are actually hurting themselves as much as, if not more than, others as a result. The flip side is, when we choose to make decisions consistent with balance and growth, the positive potential for our individual lives and our family's legacy is truly incredible. If one remains committed to making helpful choices that benefit both self and others, there truly is no limit to the blessings which can be created for all.

As optimistic as I am about the power of our free will and the impact of making positive wellness choices, I'm not going to be one of those guys trying to sell the church, or anyone for that matter, the lie that somehow, we are all going to eventually figure it out individually and create some utopia where everything works and we're all balanced and at peace. Quite the opposite actually. The world is broken and everything is not going to be fixed perfectly until Jesus returns. I believe we should continue however to do our best to fight back against all of the dysfunction, chaos, death, and destruction, despite the eventuality of the demise of this present world, if for no other reason than that God receives glory as we persist. I do believe that we should continue to do our best to be fruitful, multiply, do good works, and to do our best to live our lives to the fullest extent, helping as many people as possible to do the same, and to produce fruit for the kingdom of God by sharing the gospel of Jesus Christ as long as we can until this age ends. But be aware of false teachers, and know that this wellness message has been high-jacked by deceiving spirits; there are those who will try to convince you that somehow, people are going to be able to continue making improvements until we reach this perfect balance and create heaven on earth. Some will go so far as to promise that humans are going to figure out how to avoid death entirely! This is a lie straight from Satan. From the beginning, he has tried to get us to believe the lie that we can be like God; that we can make our own rules and live forever.

Sadly, many Christians recognize the doomed fate of our flesh, and of this current world, and determine that any effort spent to improve our temporal state is somehow a futile sin. These Christians are disrespecting the holy temple of God Almighty! With our new covenant God doesn't dwell in a temple of bricks and stone. He dwells IN US. WE are His temple. How do you think the Master feels when His servants don't keep the gates in repair? How do you think He feels when you leave His temple with broken windows and the doors wide open? Why have you let the roof cave in, allowing water to poor in, and mold and mildew to grow on priceless curtains? I could keep going with the metaphors but you get the point. Honor the God you claim to serve by presenting the vessel He gifted to you in its best maintained and most usable state. This is not to say each person is supposed to be a bodybuilder or accomplish Ironman competitions. We've all been gifted with different talents and abilities, and placed in different environments working with different variables. What I'm saying is: be a diligent steward of your specific circumstances in accordance to God's will for your life. Above everything BE OBEDIENT TO HIM. Seek an intimate, active, personal relationship with your creator and savior, the Lord Jesus Christ of Nazareth, and ask and keep asking Him to lead you, guide you, and show you the specific assignments He has for you. My goal with this book is to offer you a battle plan to accomplish just that, obedience to God and excellent completion of your specific race. We are in a war. Eternity is at stake for billions of souls, including yours. What you do with your time here matters, and since eternity is at stake, you and your decisions actually have infinite value. You build treasure in heaven based on your performance here. What level of honor do you seek? What will be your contribution to the Father's glory? I'm going to continue to encourage you to choose wellness. Choose to fight for the fulfillment of the potential given to you by our Father, here and now in this earthly vessel. Fulfill your calling with excellence and complete your assignments. Bless the Father by doing everything you can to bless as many of His children as possible. This is accomplished when you hone yourself into the sharpest, most useful tool possible. This game of life IS the pursuit of wellness whether you recognize it yet or not. All of your hopes and dreams are wrapped up in this idea, and carefully studying the playing field (or battle field) and understanding the tools and tactics of the game helps to increase your likelihood of success or victory. So, don't be lazy or complacent. Pick up your sword and your hammer; get to work and go to battle. Everything depends on your level of engagement. God doesn't need our help, but He is offering you relationship, an adventure, and the potential for honor. By the time you finish reading this book series, you will be fully equipped, and hopefully inspired, to make the most of the priceless and narrow window of opportunity that is your life.

So far in this chapter, we have mostly spent time discussing how a focus on wellness (or lack thereof) will impact your life. We've basically looked at life as an opportunity for contribution, influence, and abundance here on earth, and in eternity. We've started to understand that we are active participants, that we have some level of responsibility, and power to influence outcomes. We're almost ready to focus on the individual components of wellness and unpack the practical things we can do to make improvements in each area. To fully appreciate the different components of wellness and the significant impact each component has on the others, it will be valuable for some people to process the idea with the use of visual aids.

When I was first introduced to the wellness concept in college, they promoted what they called the "Wellness Wheel" as a tool to help people understand the concept of wellness. Most of the people I have seen teach on wellness over the years since have used something similar.

Wellness Wheel

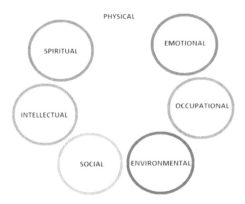

This model is useful in that it catches the eye, it's easy to read, and communicates simply the basic idea that there are more areas requiring our attention than just the physical in order to be well. I've seen variations of colors and the components moved into different areas to show that they are all equally important. I think people like the circle imagery because wellness is considered somewhat gentle and passive and soft (*however this perception is not necessarily consistent with a thorough understanding of all aspects of wellness*). The multiple colors (*eBook only, sorry!*) appeal to an interest in diversity, and show that while the components are all part of a whole, they are still able to be analyzed individually. I've seen models that show the circles overlapping, showing that the areas impact each other. All of this is good. It opens up the conversation and helps people to begin thinking about the significance of the different areas. From an instruction and assessment standpoint, I believe another model provides additional utility. I like to visualize wellness as a series of cups.

Wellness Cups

Each individual cup obviously represents each individual component of wellness. I like the use of cups for this illustration, because they are, in a sense, a vessel that can be acted upon. A cup more clearly presents opportunity for interaction than a circle. You can pour into a cup. You can pour different substances into a cup. If you pour water, for example, into a cup, you can pour a small amount, or you can pour a moderate amount. You can fill the cup to the very top, or you can pour too much and the cup would overflow. Also, regardless of the amount that you pour in, if you don't pour in any more, then the amount in the cup will eventually evaporate and the cup will be empty again. If you have a limitless amount of water, you could with some effort keep all of the cups topped off. If there is a limited amount of water with which to pour, and that amount is less than the total volume of the cups, then at that current moment it would be impossible to have all cups filled to the top. Then, you would have to choose which cups would receive more and which cups would receive less. If, after pouring into the cups, you take a step back and look and decide that you wish there to be more in one cup, you could choose to pour some from another cup. But then that cup would have less. A damaged cup with a crack in it could have a harder time holding the water and you might have to pour into it more frequently to maintain a certain level. If you're reading this book then you are probably pretty smart. The creative juices are probably starting to flow, and you are already beginning to understand where I'm going with the illustration. This model will be a useful tool to help me paint several pictures as we work our way through this I Am Well series. The better you understand this model, the more useful a tool it will be for you in your life when making decisions. It may help you to weigh the costs and benefits of a decision. It may help you to understand the impact a decision will have on your different wellness components, and therefore your life as a whole. We are also able to look at case studies with this Wellness Cup model, so we can assess and understand where a person is at from a wellness standpoint, and the impacts of their decisions across multiple wellness components. We can learn from the successes and failures of others with this model. The picture of the cups is only a snapshot in time. The levels in each cup can remain similar for entire seasons, or they can change dramatically, quickly, and often.

I find it useful with most subjects and decisions to consider them in terms of "good", "better", and "best". Obviously, the inverse of that would be "bad", "worse", and "the worst". There is, of course, an infinite number of other possibilities within those spectrums, but this will get us close enough to find meaning/ understanding, and to make meaningfully helpful decisions. For the purposes of this cup illustration, we will say that a cup which is nearly empty is the "good" situation. I say that it's good because we should be thankful that it's not completely empty! It could be worse, and any amount in the cup is helpful and a blessing, so we praise God for it!

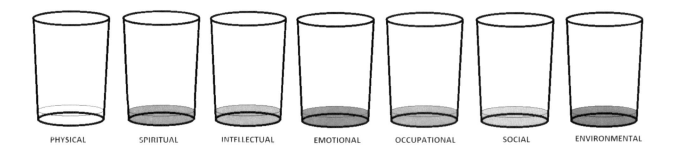

We will say that a cup which is half-full (or half-empty) is the "better" situation.

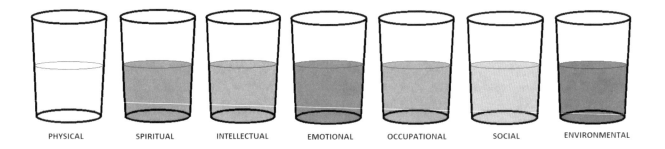

And a full cup represents a component of wellness that is functioning optimally.

This is the best-case scenario for a wellness component.

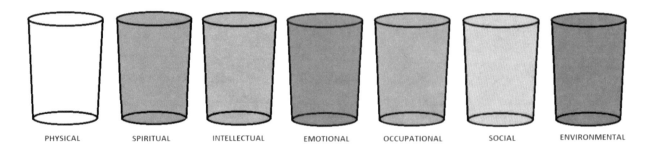

While the "full cup" picture is theoretically ideal, and is a righteous goal, I would argue that it is practically impossible in this present reality to have all seven components poured into precisely and perfectly so that you are completely and perfectly well. Normally, even the most gifted and diligent among us will have some area that still leaves room for improvement. It's possible of course through ignorance for someone to perceive all of their cups as being full even when they aren't, especially if they have never experienced a full cup in a specific area. You could come up with lots of examples, but let's go with an easy one; let's say someone is content with their environment in an impoverished third world war-stricken country because they have never experienced anything different/ better. Just because they don't know anything different, doesn't mean that their life wouldn't actually be better if they had access to clean drinking water, and/or had a safe dwelling under which to lay down their head at night. Similarly, just because someone thinks they are fine spiritually because they have a sense of being connected with nature when they hike, that doesn't mean that they are as "full" spiritually as someone who has a deep, intimate relationship with the one true God. You may have a hard time convincing the person that there is more, but once they experience the difference, then they are able to clearly identify and appreciate the greater fullness of the latter condition. You could come up with examples for all of the areas. Even if someone was somehow able to get all of their cups nearly full and completely balanced, maintaining that balance would be nearly impossible because the assignments, tools, and variables are constantly changing. There are many moving targets to hit. We all understand this on some level. Whether through diligence (or even in spite of complete negligence), we all have times where things are working better in our lives than others and we seem to be more at peace; we have seasons that are easier or more enjoyable, and seasons which are harder. My argument is, that by taking the time to educate yourself on the different areas of wellness, and becoming proficient at maintaining "better" or "best" levels, you greatly increase your odds of becoming a candidate for blessing, and for experiencing more "full" seasons, and fewer "empty" seasons. It's also true, that in God's perfect wisdom and sovereignty, He allows or even causes some cups to remain less than full for a specific purpose. Maybe there is a lesson you need to learn to qualify for a larger cup? Maybe in your honest effort to maintain a full cup you are in danger of making one cup an idol? The easiest example to share would be someone who is so obsessed with maintaining what they believe to be a perfect physical physique, that they begin to make their body an idol. They workout 24/7, obsess over their diet, and all they think about day and night is how "good" they look. That effort came at the cost of them not going to their weekly church service, their weekly small group or Bible study, doing the bare minimum at work so they can spend more time at the gym, spending all of their money on supplements and food, and neglecting spending time with their family or significant other. The goal of maximizing a full cup physically greatly diminished their overall wellness since occupational, social, and spiritual components all took a negative hit. So, if God is outside of time and can see the future and see that obsession leading the person toward dysfunction or worse, it is actually the kindness of God to allow or cause an event in their life that helps them to step back, prioritize, and balance. That "random" injury that frustrated you so much and shook you out of your obsessive fitness season was actually a blessing when you took a moment to step back, and looked at your overall life so that you could re-prioritize to improve other components. The challenge is trying to pour the correct amount of energy or intentionality into each cup, as seasons change and variables shift.

We "pour into our cups" when we are making decisions, and executing actions that are consistent with a component functioning optimally. We will dive into lots of specifics to give you ideas and coaching on helpful decisions which are indeed consistent with a component functioning optimally throughout this book series. A quick and simple example to illustrate the "pouring" metaphor here could be sleep. The decision to rest and sleep daily pours into every component, but most greatly pours into improving the physical component. A "good" idea would be to get some sleep. Any sleep. One hour is "better" than none. Will one hour of sleep provide as many benefits as four hours? Obviously not. Four hours of sleep would be "better" than one. The precise amount of sleep which produces the "best" result actually varies person by person. For some it may be 7 hours, for some it may be 8. Or it could be another number if you are an outlier. The point right now is not to deliberate the exact amount of sleep you need, but instead to illustrate that there is indeed a number that is best for you *(we will go in greater depth on sleep to help you discover your number later in this series in the I Am Physical chapter)*. The more frequently and consistently you hit that correct number, the more benefits you will experience. Getting less than the correct amount, even once, will create a detrimental effect. Getting less than the correct amount frequently, or even habitually, will produce increasingly detrimental effects. It's also possible to pour too much into a cup. If you are built to benefit the most from, say, 8 hours of sleep, and you decide to sleep for ten hours, you're not actually benefiting more from the extra hours, and in fact you can begin to cause detrimental effects to several wellness components when you do. There are some exceptions when an overflowing cup can have some benefits that we will go into later. But for the most part (with regard to this teaching illustration) you want to optimize your "pour" so that the cup is full, but not overflowing. At a minimum, even if there is not a significant detriment to an area by overflowing a cup (perhaps you don't experience fatigue from oversleeping), since we are all working with limited resources, there is an opportunity cost to each and every decision we make. Even if you somehow had access to unlimited finances,

THERE IS A LIMITED AMOUNT OF TIME IN EACH DAY.

This single truth creates most of the tension and stress we battle. Our God (Father, Son, and Holy Spirit) is the only uncreated being. He always was, He is, and He always will be. Literally everything else was created by Him and for Him. All created things are affected by time. All created things have limited power, limited knowledge, and limited utility. We all have handicaps when compared to the one and only all-powerful God. These handicaps create a beautiful dilemma: the opportunity for failure, the opportunity to get it wrong, and the opportunity to run out of time. Until Jesus came in the flesh, this was the one glory we shared collectively apart from the Father: the opportunity to get it right in the face of the possibility to get it wrong. Before Jesus put on flesh and came to earth, He was perfect and incapable of imperfection. It was literally impossible for Him to make a wrong decision. Then He came, chose to put on flesh, and allowed Himself to be tempted. He was the only one to live a sinless life in spite of all of life's wretched temptations and trials. If you're reading this, then you are still here, in your flesh, lacking omniscience, and running out of time and strength each day. From the beginning, we have all worked with the same amount of time in a day, and yet some people are able to accomplish much more than others. True, some are gifted more and granted a head start. But we often see many who started out ahead end terribly far behind. We also see plenty of examples of people who defy all odds and create a life full of accomplishments that change the course of history, who began much further behind than most. There is therefore an urgent necessity to make "full cup" choices, consistently, right now. People in finance understand concepts called "time-value-of-money", and "compounding interest". A dollar from today will be worth less in the future if it is left under your mattress, due to inflation. But a dollar invested today will produce an exponential return, and each day that the dollar is not invested costs you more and more. The same is true regarding wellness. We have but a short time to invest our talents and to make the right choices to maximize ourselves as instruments of the Lord. In most cases, the sooner you get your stuff together the longer you will have to seek Him and find Him in deeper and deeper places. Ultimately, after having proven yourself with smaller things, you are trusted with larger and larger assignments. Starting sooner, in most cases, will result in a more impressive resume of successes, and should produce greater kingdom fruit. Of course, the Lord can break the rules He has established in this place. He can part seas. He can raise the dead. And He can pour out His spirit and grace, and anoint an 11th hour worker to do greater exploits than someone who has walked with Him for 50 years. That case would be an exception though, not the rule. The more you begin to understand the true weight of each decision you make, down to the seemingly small and insignificant, the more you become present to the awareness that literally every choice is a plus or a negative. Every choice is either consistent with accomplishing a goal, or it isn't. There is no gray area. Sometimes there can be a lack of understanding that can make a decision difficult to determine, but even if we lack understanding, the choice still has an impact. Every decision, thought, word, and action impacts both the physical and the spiritual worlds. Ultimately, every decision, thought, word, choice and action therefore have some level of value toward the eternal. Every choice is either moving you closer to order, or closer to chaos. Every choice is either creating life, or destroying it, on some level. Every choice, therefore, is either serving the kingdom of God, or serving the kingdom of Satan. Choose you this day whom you will serve (you have done this every day since you were born, and will continue to do this every day for the rest of your life through your choices, whether you acknowledge it or not). I know this all can seem extreme, and the language used so far has seemed somewhat intense. For some people, this would cause them to look at the message I am trying to share as a burden that would steal all of the enjoyment out of life. Quite the opposite is true! Managing your wellness with intentionally wise decisions is indeed a burden, but it is one that produces more and more joy as you become willing to carry more and more of the burden! Seek first the kingdom of God and His righteousness, and then all these things shall be added unto you. When you are really getting this wellness thing right, you are actually experiencing greater joy, greater peace, a greater sense of satisfaction, and you experience more self-worth. The great news is, you don't have to wait until the end of your life to experience some of the benefits of choosing to be responsible around managing your choices. Normally, there is an immediate improvement or blessing in your life, or in the life of someone you love, when you make the right choice. If you haven't been physically active and you go for just a 10-minute walk, you immediately feel better. These small wins help you to stay in the battle and make more "better" and "best" level decisions. It's also true that the longer and more consistently you make those better decisions, you tend to experience even greater rewards. It's good to get a good job. Staying with that job and consistently doing what it takes to level up there, in theory, should eventually produce greater results, greater rewards, and greater freedom. Another illustration that is helpful in understanding the significance of making "better" and "best" level decisions sooner, and with greater consistency throughout your life, is a simple line which we will look at next.

Order vs Chaos and the Snowball Effect

Life/ wellness can be looked at in terms of a line with chaos on one end and order on the other. It's true that the lines go on forever in each direction. Your experience will be vastly different depending on where you are on this line. A life spent in order will result in blessing, while a life of chaos creates suffering, the degree to which depends on how far you go in each direction.

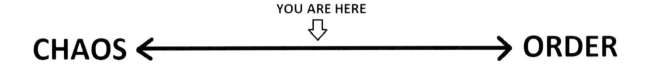

It's all about how well things work. This model is true on both micro and macro levels. The macro level would include your entire life as a whole. You could of course consider larger and larger scales beyond yourself, but for the purposes of this book we are going to focus on yourself, since that is where you have the most control. But as a concept, you could of course consider the entire world being the largest macro line in the physical sense (being limited by flesh, time, and space). The truest line includes the afterlife, once our flesh dies and our spirit lives for eternity. But we start with the decisions we are making here and now in this flesh, in this arena, on this battlefield. The more everyone is working together, building each other up, contributing, and serving each other, we are able to accomplish bigger and better things. If a society trends away from order toward chaos, then there is less coordination among the individual parts, things don't work as well, and we are collectively able to accomplish less. It's simpler of course to look at the micro level. Let's consider a car. It has many different parts that all have to work together for all of the features to work. The car is still a car if it has a flat tire, but its utility has greatly decreased if you're unable to move. As more and more components fail, the vehicle is able to offer less to the user. The longer the vehicle's repairs are neglected, the greater the effort and cost there will be to restore it to its most useful state. If you focus enough destructive energy toward the vehicle, it eventually becomes truly unsalvageable scrap metal, and its life as a vehicle has ended. The same is true with us. Our physical bodies are vessels, providing a place where our spirits and souls temporarily reside. We have tremendous utility in our bodies. The range of capabilities of the human body is miraculous really. But we have to operate our vehicle within the confines of the rules of the system. Your bones can only hold a certain amount of weight. Your brain can only produce a limited amount of electricity. You are only able to focus on, and accomplish, a finite number of tasks. We can break our components and then our vessel doesn't provide as much utility. Sometimes, we are able to repair damages and even make improvements along the way to increase the utility available. Sadly though, most people treat their bodies like the neglected car. They don't change the oil. The belts and hoses are worn. Most people don't even do the simple regular routine maintenance, much less making any improvements to increase performance. I know this is a long intro, but stay with me and we will eventually get to more of the tangible dos and don'ts with helpful, practical tips for routine maintenance and performance enhancements. But of more value than a simple list of a few tasks is the mindset, awareness, and understanding of the true concept of wellness, hence the belaboring of points here and sharing of different analogies, metaphors, and multiple illustrations. The tangible task lists also sometimes change over time as knowledge increases, new technology is introduced, and our variables change. If I only gave you a list of a few dos and don'ts, you would be ill equipped to survive in a changing environment. If you truly master this concept of wellness, then technically, you will continue to persist, thrive, and find balance in an ever-changing environment. Please hang in here with me a little longer and allow me the honor of continuing to try to articulate what wellness is, and how to get it right, before we move on to the daily fleshly tangible recommendations. Seriously, continue to choose to focus and process what I'm saying here. Make the connections. Put the pieces together. Create synapsis. We are trying to increase our level of wisdom from which to process information so that you are able to move toward discernment and creativity, rather than being limited to the experiences and creativity of someone who means well, but was created differently than you for different purposes. We need to help you get dialed in to who *you* were specifically created to be, so you know how to fine tune *your* machine (you).

Continuing with the Order vs Chaos illustration:

On the chaos side you have the works of the flesh. Unfortunately, the sin disease we inherited from Adam and Eve gave us a propensity toward choices which create death, meaning that we don't really even have to try that hard to destroy our lives and/or the lives of others. It's somewhat natural to us. It's our default. It's actually somewhat unnatural to make decisions consistent with order. We have to learn which decisions are consistent with order and life, and then we have to learn the discipline to continue making more and more of those unnatural, healthy, order-decisions. Just look at a baby; they don't know what is good for them to put in their mouth, and what is bad for them to put in their mouths. If they were left in their ignorance, most of them would probably choke on something. The toddler without instruction would run into traffic, or touch the hot stove, out of ignorance and natural curiosity. We want to see what happens. Even when we're told not to, and told there will be consequences, we still want to see for ourselves. The mercy of God protects us like a good parent who protects their children as they are learning. Eventually though, the child is expected to have the basics down and to begin to take on more complex responsibilities. When we master our part with the smaller responsibilities, we become qualified to be trusted to take on larger responsibilities as we move further and further toward order. The child is eventually trusted with scissors, glue, and paint, and eventually they create works of art. The art they create gets more and more complex and beautiful, as they get more and more skilled at using the art tools. On the order side, we all enjoy more benefits. On the chaos side, we have fewer and fewer options until eventually everything collapses. On the order side, creativity and life spring forth. On the chaos side of the spectrum, you find destruction and ultimately death. Again, it's all about how well things work. On the order side, the pieces fit together and things work. On the chaos side, things don't fit together well, and they simply don't work. The fate of a flower is a simple example. For a flower to grow it needs what? Soil, water, sunlight, a seed, and then a little miracle life force blessing from God. If all of those pieces are there in the right amount, at the right times, then the flower will grow and produce more flowers. If you start messing with any of those ingredients, the health of the flower begins to suffer and eventually, if there is enough chaos, the flower dies. We are magnificently more complex than the flower, so we have many more variables to manage. This creates a greater variety of fruit/results that are possible as the variables interact with each other. If you have ever taken a moment to consider the complexity of even a simple combination lock, and the total number of possible combinations you have from just a few numbers, you begin to have an appreciation for the exponential possibilities that become available as you add in thousands of "numbers" or variables, of which many are constantly changing! You really begin to have a great appreciation (*even with our miniscule understanding*) of the complex and truly miraculous nature of life. The greater your understanding of just how many variables there are out there, and that somehow most of them are interacting together in beneficial and orderly ways, the idea that all of this is random becomes nearly statistically impossible. There has to be an architect or a designer. That's why you are finally seeing brilliant atheists beginning to shift from the lame argument that everything we are is an accident that came from nothing, to that there is some sort of intelligence that put this into order. The tragedy is, most still refuse to humble themselves before the Almighty sovereign God. They would rather believe that we were seeded by aliens, but all that does is kick the can a little further down the road and ignore the question, "then who created them?". Eventually, no matter how far back you want to kick the can of cause and effect, you eventually are confronted with the question, "where did the original matter come from?" And there's never a satisfactory answer to the flesh, because it's not really a physical question. There is no way for us to comprehend any being that always was, is, and always will be. But that is the reality of the situation. Fight it as much as you want, you will never find a satisfactory answer in the flesh. I find the idea interesting that God could one day explain that reality to us in a way that we understand. The situation we find ourselves in presently, however, is that we were created. We had a birthday and there will be a day that our physical life ends. So, let's focus on what to do with the time in-between. The nearly infinite combination of variables, experiences, and choices available to us all, even within our limited lifespan, provide a truly beautiful tapestry when you weave all of our lives together. Be the best thread you can be. Contribute beauty to your small corner. You do that when you live a life of order. You do that when you resist the works of the flesh, and deny the enemy the satisfaction of creating chaos.

All of this talk about order and chaos really helps to take the emotions out of our decision-making process, and helps us to bring the flesh into submission. When you are able to take a step back and look at the decision you are about to make, you can ask yourself, "Does this decision move my life closer toward chaos, or closer to order?" or "Is this decision consistent with progress and achieving a goal, or is it not?" It's literally always one or the other.

Every decision you make is ultimately moving you in one direction or the other on this Order vs Chaos line. You are literally always in motion on this spectrum; you are never simply standing still. Some decisions only move you a short distance, while others are more impactful and can move you further. Some decisions are so terrible that you move miles toward chaos, and set yourself back so far that it takes years to recover. Others are such terrible decisions that the result is death and the end of this physical game. The positive side works the same. You can make lots of little decisions that are helpful to improving your overall level of wellness over time. You are also given the opportunity to make big improvement-decisions, however those opportunities are usually rare in a person's life. Marrying the right spouse, for example, would qualify as one of these rare major-impact improvement-decisions. The part most people find difficult about mastering this dichotomy is that life seems to be an uphill battle. Success in the flesh can require millions of solid "order" decisions, sometimes overcoming great adversity with massive difficulty for seemingly small benefit, while the opportunities to take huge leaps toward chaos are easy, plentiful, usually masterfully deceptive, and often extremely tempting. Massive chaos can be achieved with little to no effort, while achieving marginal levels of order can require tremendous discipline and sustained effort for long durations. When you consider the disproportionate weight that chaos decisions have in your life verses the weight of order decisions, the line begins to look more like this:

Life and wellness, then, can be looked at like a snowball. Life is always "snowballing" in one direction or another. When you start a new series of decisions, you push the snowball in one direction. It's moving slowly at first. When you keep making those same decisions you are pushing the snowball harder and harder. It begins to increase in size and picks up momentum.

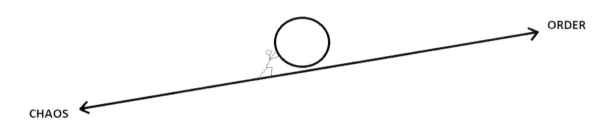

The snowball only has two options, forward or backwards. Continuing to push your snowball toward order helps you to gain momentum. It builds up strength, so that when you hit bumps you are not slowed down as much. The better disciplined you are for longer periods of time helps you to build up momentum so that you are not affected as severely by a negative choice. Example: say you have been consistent with a strict, healthier diet for 6 months, and then you decide to have a massive bowl of ice cream. Is that ice-cream helpful? Well, maybe emotionally to a degree if it makes you happy, but that might be temporary if you become sad about it when you feel terrible and bloated later physically. But if your healthy diet habits are strong, you recover fairly quickly from the poor decision and begin to make those good decisions again. Compare that to someone who has just decided it's time to make a change in their diet for the better. They are weak and vulnerable to temptation. They haven't yet seen successes which create belief in themselves, and they have not yet experienced the benefits of the discipline, to know that they value the discipline more than the temporary perceived benefit of giving in to their fleshly temptation. They are more easily deceived and discouraged. The same decision to eat the same bowl of ice cream could affect the second person differently. Rather than feeling bad for an hour, drinking some water, and then going back to the healthy habits that are normal for the first person, the second person could believe the lie that "they don't have the strength to continue this commitment, and it's probably not worth it anyway". They go back for a second bowl and the downward spiral toward chaos continues. The second person continues to suffer in poor health and remains in bondage to their flesh. Hence the importance of training your children to make healthy wellness decisions from an early age. When they have grown up in order, and the benefits are a normal experience to them, if they ever do make poor decisions, they will feel the difference and desire personally to get back to where things work and feel better. It's much easier to maintain an excellent level of wellness than it is to rescue a person deep in chaos. The more time spent in chaos, the more time, effort, and discipline it will take to get a person up the hill with enough forward momentum so they are staying on the path toward wellness no matter what life throws at them.

The other easy illustration is of course using the analogy of a fruit bearing tree. Decisions consistent with order deepen the root system. Decisions consistent with chaos cause the roots to wither. Order "roots" efficiently deliver water and nutrients to the tree. Eventually the trunk is large enough to support big branches. Eventually fruit is produced. The longer that tree continues to deepen its root system, the stronger the trunk, the more numerous the branches, and the bigger, more numerous, and more delicious the fruit.

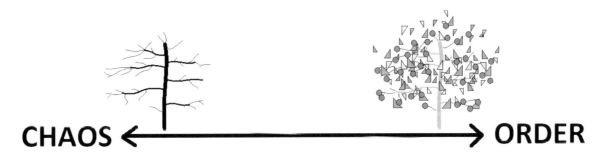

You should get the point by now. Your decisions are important. Making decisions consistent with order produces life (the full life you really want, and the life God designed for you). Making decisions consistent with chaos produces less joy, fewer options, and ultimately death. If we want to bring back our wellness cups, we would see them fall on our line like this:

Or more accurately:

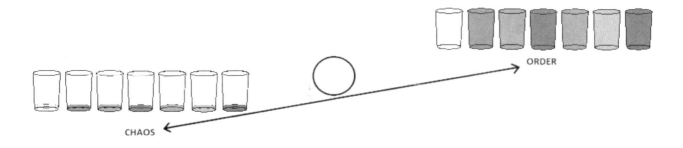

You know… it's funny; for 20 years I have thought about these wellness illustrations. That whole time, I thought the original Wellness Wheel was just a less-thought-through model that provided less utility than the cups. As I was writing this chapter though, they finally all just came together.

You can actually consider the circles of the Wellness Wheel to be an aerial view of the cups!

As a younger man I spent some time as a waiter serving tables. We had a drink tray that was a circle. If I needed to bring many drinks to a table, I would need to space them out evenly on the tray to make them easier to carry, and to reduce the chance of accidentally dropping the tray (chaos). Similarly, with wellness, we need to balance the cups to make the burden easier to carry.

You hear people use the saying "30,000 ft view" when they want to discuss an idea or project broadly, as if you are flying above something and looking down. If you flew over a building, you would just be able to make out the basic shape of the building, the roof, and some general details. They want you to begin to understand the bigger picture before you get closer to the specific details.

This, then, would be the 30,000 ft fly-over view of wellness using the cups:

Once you land the plane and get on the ground level you are able to see way more details. As you approach the building on foot, you see it from the side. You are able to see where to enter the building. You are able to begin to size up the effort it would require to reach the top level i.e., how many stair cases might be inside etc. This, then, is more of a ground level view of the Wellness Wheel:

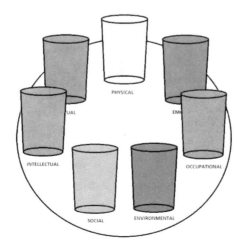

I had a really fun time doing our photo session for the book cover artwork. I actually found some cups, a pitcher, and a serving tray that worked nicely. At first, I was slightly disappointed that the tray I bought was too small to recreate the diagram I just shared exactly, but then I saw things slightly differently, and just like every time God switches things up on us, it ended up being better than I originally hoped.

The cups I bought fit perfectly on the tray, as long as one cup was in the center. Instantly, I knew which cup belonged there. You may already be able to guess, but by the time you finish reading this I Am Well series, I'm sure that you will strongly agree with me that our spiritual cup is central, and ultimately the most important. All of the other cups are visible to the physical eyes, with spirituality usually remaining invisible and inside everything else. If you had to choose just one cup to pour into, it would be the spiritual, and as you continued to pour into the spiritual, it would overflow and bless all of the others. Praise the Lord!

Most of the remaining chapters in this I Am Well series will focus on details of how to "fill" each respective cup, and how to balance them on your tray. Rather than just looking at the "building" from the outside, we will go inside and begin to analyze the structure. We will learn the floorplan, and begin the process of becoming more efficient at living inside the building that we have initially only flown over. Upon completion of this series, you will be able to survive and thrive in the building. You will understand how everything works and how you fit in. Then you will be able to get creative, start decorating the house, and making it more uniquely yours. You will know how to fill <u>your</u> cups.

There is another metaphor that will be helpful as we navigate the tough topics in this book. I first heard this illustration taught by Pastor Dean Odle from Fire and Grace Church in Opelika, Alabama. I like it, and will use this illustration often throughout this series. Our journey to find truth is a road. On both sides of any truth there are errors that people fall into, like the ditches on either side of a road.

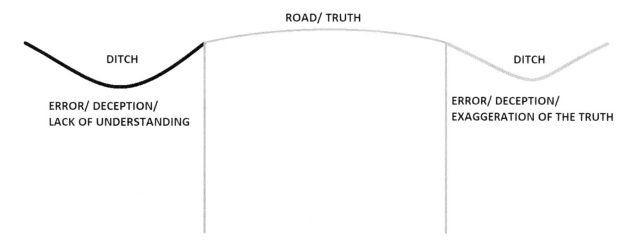

There's much more you could put in the list of errors on each side of the ditch, but you get the point. There is truth. Often times, in the effort to find and walk in truth, we recognize one error, and while trying to stay as far away from that ditch, we end up falling into the other. In the later chapters, when I begin sharing what is true on many different topics, I will shed light on some of the errors on either side of each truth. I'll try to expose the ditches, so hopefully we stay out of the ditches and stay on the road to truth!

Enter ye in at the strait gate: for wide is the gate, and broad is the way, that leadeth to destruction, and many there be which go in thereat: Because strait is the gate, and narrow is the way, which leadeth until life, and few there be that find it.

Matthew 7:13-14

Going forward in life it will always be wise when you are seeking truth, or when someone else points to a ditch, to be aware that there are usually ditches on both sides of the real truth, and you need to avoid falling into either trap to truly fill your cup. It is important to fill your cup with truth. Attempting to fill your cup with lies unfortunately doesn't fill up the cup. Lies are more like poison or acid that contaminate the good fluid in your cup and try to eat holes in the cup, so that cup is less capable of holding good liquid in the future.

FILLING YOUR CUP WITH TRUTH

ATTEMPTING TO FILL YOUR CUP WITH LIES

The Healer can heal and repair holes in your cup that were caused by pouring in lies, but pouring more acid or poison, even if it is a different type, will just cause more holes and more chaos. Better than praying for a healed cup is to avoid poison in the first place! But, if you have a cup which has been damaged, the good news is, God still uses damaged vessels. When He heals you, those cracks can become stronger than they were before, and the former weaknesses can become strengths. Often, we see where God uses someone who was previously terribly broken to minister to those who are in the place where that person used to be. You know how to find someone who is in a place where you are familiar. Just don't get too comfortable in those old places. Snatch someone out and give them some healthy truth to pour in if you can, but do not accept poison again, even in an attempt to rescue someone further down the chaos spectrum. Only order can rescue someone from chaos. More chaos can only produce... you guessed it, more chaos. Abstain from evil therefore. Be obedient to God. Resist the devil, and he will flee from you.

We really could keep going with analogy after analogy, and metaphor after metaphor, but I don't want to lose your interest. Eventually we need to move on from talking about the concept of wellness and its importance, and we need to shift into talking about how to actually maximize each component/ fill each cup. Are you starting to grasp the concept of wellness I am describing? Are you starting to form a working definition of wellness from which to work? Do you have the context of the different wellness components? Are you beginning to appreciate the interdependencies among them? Are you beginning to understand the importance of maximizing each area by pouring in truth and maintaining a full cup? Are you beginning to resolve to press toward order? Are you beginning to commit yourself to the endeavor of fleeing from chaos? Will you keep pushing the snowball uphill until it gains momentum, such that you begin to experience more order and therefore more wellness?

I hope so!

28

So... what is wellness?

Wellness can be broken down into seven components:

1. Physical
2. Spiritual
3. Intellectual
4. Emotional
5. Occupational
6. Social
7. Environmental

What else is Wellness?

- Wellness is a verb
- Wellness is a noun
- Wellness is the battlefield where we fight Satan for the full life God planned for us
- Wellness is a multi-prong attack in this spiritual war
- Wellness is the current status of where we are in the battle
- Wellness is the outward symptom or manifestation of invisible conditions
- Wellness is the symphony of many complex systems
- Wellness is a finely tuned utility vessel, and the relationship between the pilot/ driver and the machine/craft/vessel
- Wellness is the declaration of a blessing
- Wellness is a temporary location-place-marker on the infinite line-continuum of chaos and order
- Wellness is the goal
- Wellness is the prize
- Wellness is the acceptance of truth and rejection of lies
- Wellness is a life fully surrendered in repentance and obedience to the Lord Jesus Christ of Nazareth, and the continuing courageous sacrifice of your life as a true servant
- Wellness pulls you from eternal fire and the damnation of chaos, and pushes you toward the eternal life offered from submission to order

So, when you see someone and they ask, "how are you?" and you respond, "I am well!" you could mean several different things. Technically, anytime you say you are well you are telling the truth simply by being alive. Once you gain understanding that there are multiple combinations possible of varying levels of fullness in the different wellness cups, you understand that where you are on the wellness continuum is always shifting.

What someone should ask if they are truly interested in your present condition is:

"How well are you?"

or,

"Which of your wellness cups are full, and which are empty? Why is that their current status? Is there anything I can do to help you pour into the deficient cups?"

Ok, I get that is weird and nobody talks like that, I'm just dissecting the language and the implied meaning.

By the end of this I Am Well series, when someone asks how you are doing and you reply, "I am well", what I hope you will sincerely mean is:

"I am diligently managing the pouring into of all seven of my components of wellness. I am content with, thankful for, and owning responsibility for the current levels in each of my wellness cups!"

At a minimum, anytime you hear the word, "well", or "wellness", I hope it causes you to remember that you play an active role in the managing of your cups, and that there is always an opportunity to push the snowball toward order. I hope you recognize the exponential possibilities present to you at any given moment, and I hope you will choose to engage in the battle. So, when you say, "I am well", it is a declaration that you are still in the battle, striving for better balance and victory against the kingdom of darkness.

The tragic reality is, when most people answer "I'm well thank you", they're actually lying. The truth for most people is that several components are needing attention, and several cups are cracked, nearly dry, and desperately requiring work to be filled. My goal is that by reading this series, it won't be long before you are indeed authentically telling the truth about your present state when you say, "I am well".

As with everything, generations of intense, scientific study and technological advancements eventually produce the results that the Bible has taught all along. The Bible has taught us about wellness, just in slightly different terms. In many places, the Bible tells us that we are three parts, body, soul, and spirit. Really, physical, spiritual, intellectual, and emotional components of wellness are just sub-categories that fall within these three main categories of self. There is perfectly sufficient instruction in the Bible regarding occupational, social, and environmental components also. There is nothing new under the sun. I'm just doing my best to present to you my understanding of how a several-thousand-year-old living document is actually the very breath and Word of God, and hopefully to encourage you to read it/Him, study it/Him, and obey it/Him. My hope is that I am a contribution toward your realization of truth, toward your victory over the evil one, and toward your actually experiencing "life-more-abundantly". I hope to help you be well. In order to undertake this most noble task, you are going to need some tools in order to win this battle.

Free Will and Language are the first tools you will need to master in order to find victory in this wellness saga.

Chapter 2: Free Will and Language

At some point in eternity, our Heavenly Father decided that He would create. First, He created the spiritual world and angelic beings. Eventually, He decided to create the physical when He made the world, and eventually, man in His own image. In His infinite wisdom and perfect love, He created these beings with free will. We could write several books just on this one profound truth. For true love to exist there MUST be free will. Any time we hear about an act of kidnapping or rape, most people immediately experience a sense of terrible disgust. Even people who are confused into believing that morality is relative will almost unanimously agree that the concepts of forcing yourself upon someone and denying them the ability to choose for themselves is reprehensible, disgusting, wrong, to be fought against vehemently, and even violently when necessary. The damage done and chaos created from allowing a policy such a slavery to exist for example, clearly wounds and damages countless generations in ways that are impossible to fully understand. When free will is violated, suffering occurs. We know this at our core. Even if you somehow took the suffering element away and reduced life to a series of random cause and effect relationships, without free will you are left with an existence that is reduced to meaningless insignificance. I don't believe our Heavenly Father wanted to create just a random piece of art to look at. He didn't just want a painting to hang over His couch. He didn't want soul-less robots. In His infinite wisdom, perfect peace, love, righteousness, and holiness, He created real LIFE. His creation was living. When He breathed in life He breathed in real meaning. This creation of His was a living thing with moving parts. It was exciting and dynamic. Here was a real adventure. Here is a creation made in His image and after His likeness with the ability to create and destroy. Here is a creation that is both pathetically weak and vulnerable, but yet simultaneously infinitely powerful. He built into us the ability to reject Him. Seriously, pause for a second and reflect on that. The all-powerful, all-knowing, ever-present, limitless creator of everything gave us the gift, as created things, the ability to reject the one who's power cannot be tested, tried, or overcome. In a sense, He made Himself vulnerable. He opened His heart to us. He chose to love us. He chose to desire us. He chose to include us and to give us the gift of being able to choose Him. This point is so profound, that if people could really wrap their heads around what it truly means to be holy, they would understand that all of the terrible pain and suffering in the world was unfortunately necessary for true love to exist. In this sense, the pain and suffering in the world can actually be seen as beautiful, and as part of the gift. Without something to choose from/between, there is no choice, therefore no free will, therefore no meaning, and therefore no real love. For real love to exist, hate must also exist (at least temporarily). For goodness to exist and have real meaning, evil must also exist (at least temporarily). This is one of the hardest concepts for most people to grasp, and sadly one of the biggest reasons atheists reject the idea of God. They lack an understanding or appreciation for the magnificently beautiful gift that is free will, and the realities that such a profound meaning necessarily create. They focus on the negative side of the equation, rather than claiming the beautiful free gift offered to them that infinitely outweighs the cost. They also ignore or discount the fact that our Father suffers with us. He loves us and doesn't want us to suffer. It grieves Him when we grieve. He chose to take on this weight, the suffering of the entire world, just so He could share real, true, intimate love with us. Remember this when you find yourself in suffering. He not only bares your burden, but also bares all of the burdens of every other suffering person, and has shared in every suffering of every single person that has ever lived. Keeping this focus can help us to realize just how small our suffering is compared to the greatness and goodness of God. He isn't indifferent. He isn't leaving us to suffer in the middle of war, famine, disease, and/or death while He is off on some vacation. He is right there in the trenches with us every step of the way. He is eventually going to work everything beautifully for good, and we will eventually understand why all of this was necessary.

You have to understand, He gave the angels the gift of free will too, and a third of them rebelled against Him. This entire experience here on earth is designed exactly the way it needs to be for a free will eternity in heaven to be possible. No more suffering or trials than are needed is allowed. We are proving to Him right now with every moment of every day for the rest of our physical lives whether or not we are the ones who will choose Him for ALL of eternity going forward. That's why this has to be so difficult. He doesn't want those who are going to choose to love, worship, and obey Him for 100 years, 1000 years, or even 100,000 years; He is holy, and His presence cannot allow rebellion and wickedness, so He has created the perfect plan to sort out who will choose Him forever. Yes, it is quite the gauntlet. But I believe God receives more and more glory as we persist through greater and greater difficulties and resist greater and greater temptations. Not only does God receive more glory, but we are being given the gift of honor through our persistence. It is easy and immature to become frustrated with all of life's uncertainties and challenges. This fantastic Proverb has been a great comfort to me over the past few years:

It is the glory of God to conceal a thing: but the honour of kings is to search out a matter.

Proverbs 25:2

Practically, most people have some level of understanding of this concept of free will, as it pertains to choosing to believe in God or not. Most people are terribly ignorant, however, in their understanding of the depth to where this gift of free will goes, how profoundly it truly touches everything we do in life, and the tangible power in your physical life that comes from mastering your will and bringing it into submission. Yes, the most important detail of free will is spending eternity in heaven with your creator in perfect love. The power of free will also literally creates the story of your life here on earth too though. I do believe that before we were in our mother's womb, God knew us and had a plan for our life. He created us all differently, some are taller or shorter, some are more gifted in certain areas, etc. But then what we do with those variables is up to us.

We start out as babies. Yes, we are body, soul, and spirit from day one (conception). We fine tune our body and spirit as we grow. We will get into more details of mastering the body in the I Am Physical chapter. We can reiterate now though, that our bodies are just the physical vessels that house our soul and spirit. Our soul and spirit are what live forever. Our soul is who we really are. This is where the decision making takes place. This is command central and everything flows from here. We make a decision in our soul, then the spirit gives the message to the body which receives the command and does what we tell it to do. Kind of like the car analogy again, the spirit would be the one pushing the gas pedal, turning the steering wheel etc. and it's the car that touches the road. The car gives us feedback. We have gauges, etc. that tell us how much fuel we have remaining, how much electricity is charged in the battery, how fast we are going etc. Sometimes we get alerts like a check engine light, or a buzzer when we get too close to something in reverse. In all of those cases, we still have a choice in what we will do with that information. When you receive an alert that the gas has reached the lower 1/8th of the tank, you can choose to pull over and get gas, or not. You can push it a little farther, but if you keep going you will eventually run out of gas. When that check engine light comes on, you can either take the car in to the shop to diagnose the problem, or you can ignore it. Oftentimes you can go for a while without addressing the issue. It's possible though, that by ignoring the light you are potentially causing yourself greater damage and increased costs of repair. You could even choose to keep pushing the gas pedal when you sense you have a flat tire. Pretty quickly though, you will not only need a new tire but also a new wheel. Keep going and you're going to tear up even more parts.

The point here is not to keep riding the car analogy, but to illustrate that you are in control of your vehicle. Most people live their entire lives at the mercy of the whims of their flesh. Rather than their spirit powerfully controlling their body with wisdom for specific purposes, their body controls their spirit. What if your gas light comes on when you have ¾ of a tank left? If you have a long drive ahead of you and pull over every time that light comes on, the trip is going to be harder and take much longer. Time is valuable, so the trip costs you more too. You lose time that could have been spent doing a thousand other things if the time had been used efficiently. Most of us have much more fuel left in the tank than we think.

The goal then becomes gaining wisdom to know what is true regarding the capabilities of the vehicle, and how your control of the vehicle really impacts your trip and your destination. The reality is, our flesh is whiny, weak, and wicked. Most people pull their car over as soon as the engine temperature increases, not understanding that it was designed to operate well at many temperatures. Some are afraid to take their 4wd truck off of the pavement and end up missing out on going to the fun and exciting places where they could have gone. Others try to drive their 2wd truck off road, break the vehicle, and get stuck. Others try to race the family mini-van and get depressed when it doesn't perform like a sportscar. There are things we can do to manipulate the performance of the platform we were gifted, but the reality is we're stuck with what we are given. The reality too, is that what we were given is capable of much more than most people know.

The goal, again, is to gain wisdom to really know what is true when making decisions. We are in control of so much more than most people understand. I will try to unpack more of this throughout all of the successive chapters because this is huge and a critical piece to winning this game, keeping your cups full, and achieving a desirable level of wellness. We make a ton of choices that impact our physical wellness. What did you eat today, did you exercise etc.? Those are the easier choices for people to recognize, even if they only recognize that they failed to make the healthy choice. Most people fail to recognize the power of free will and their choices as it pertains to the other areas of wellness though. Are you aware that you actually control your emotions? Everything down to the most basic of responses is a choice. Some damaged individuals choose to associate pain with pleasure, and choose to enjoy cutting themselves for example. Even if this is a pretend show, they are still overriding their bodies natural response to flee from pain as they push toward the pain. They choose to relate to the pain as something they desire. Obviously, this is a destructive example but the same concept can be used for good. If our flesh is wicked and we are susceptible to laziness, selfishness, and lies, then being able (as sovereign souls) to take control of our weak flesh by our spirit to command the body to do what we want it to do can produce benefits in our lives. Forcing yourself to do your homework, or to wake up early and take a shower before going to work, rather than getting an extra 30 minutes of sleep like your body wants, are clear examples of times when pushing yourself through areas where your body's senses are creating obstacles and telling you to stop are beneficial. The goal, then, is to gain as much wisdom, in as many areas as you can, so that you avoid the ditches on either side of the truth on each area. Avoid not doing enough, but also avoid doing too much. Find the spot in your decision making where the decisions you make are "just right" and produce "porridge" which is neither too hot nor too cold. The greater you understand just how powerful your will is, when it is appropriate to use the incredible power of your free will to make and complete a choice which may seem difficult or impossible, and when you need to dial it back and not force your will, you will begin to accomplish tasks and series of tasks which others find impressive and out of their reach. You begin to create balance. Your root system grows deeper. Your branches stretch out further. You become able to absorb more nutrients, weather more storms, and produce more and better fruit.

This is really just an introduction to the concept of free will and choice as being something over which you are in control, but I hope to give you greater understanding of just how powerful you are, and the degree to which you are in control of each and every individual component of wellness, as we work our way through the remainder of this series. You have to get this concept down though. You have to start to believe that you are an active participant in your story, and in His story. You have to start to take extreme ownership of your life and everything around you. You are in control of so much more than you understand. Believing the lie that you are a complete victim to your circumstances keeps a person weak, vulnerable, and ineffective. It keeps a person in bondage to the lazy, deceitful, selfish, wicked meat-suit they have to wear here, and at the mercy of the evil meat-suits of other people. This is why we are supposed to bring our flesh into submission. Yes, to avoid sin and say "no" to the things we should say "no" to, but also at times we have to force ourselves into obedience to do the things that we should do! If the Lord tells you to go mow your elderly neighbor's lawn when you're tired and you just want to relax, you have to force your body to do what it doesn't want to do, if you are to be found in obedience. Everything worth doing normally has some degree of difficulty or sacrifice involved. There are some people who will choose to do the hard things the Lord commands them to, and there are those who refuse due to fear or laziness. Either way, the obedient servant (the one connected to the vine) produces meaningful fruit, and the slothful servant (who does nothing with his or her talent) produces nothing. Sadly, by producing nothing you are actually producing death. *(Remember the uphill battle that is wellness. If you are not conquering new territory and gaining victories, then this corrupted world is allowed to destroy you. Without diligence you will be overcome. Kind of like how inflation affects the purchasing power of a dollar. A dollar will be worth less and able to accomplish less tomorrow than it can today, so there is wisdom is creating today so that you continue to maintain forward progress tomorrow, and the next day, as the world and other people move forward. The servants of Satan are busy creating destruction, so we must be proactive to promote life, otherwise we will be overcome. "All that is necessary for evil to prosper is that good men do nothing" right?)* This principle of mastering your will helps you to be better at resisting the destructive temptations of the flesh, and simultaneously helps you to maximize your effectiveness and efficiency at being the best servant/most useful tool that you can be for the kingdom of God, for your family, and ultimately for yourself too.

I've owned several dogs over the course of my life. Some absolutely loved to play fetch and would retrieve the ball no matter how tired they were, and no matter how many times I would throw it. Other dogs of mine couldn't care less, and would refuse with complete disinterest. Both the obedient and the disobedient were fully capable of choosing to move their legs and to go get me the ball. Which dogs do you think I enjoyed more? Which dogs got more attention? Which ones did I interact with more? Which dogs did I invest more time into teaching more tricks? Obviously, we're more valuable than dogs, and our Heavenly Father is a much better "owner" than I, but you get the point. Be willing to engage. Be willing to do the assignments which are assigned to you. Do them with enthusiasm! Do them with excellence! If you are faithful in a small thing, you will be faithful in a larger thing. Most people claim they are interested in having a life of significance, but when you really get down to it, they aren't willing to choose to do what that life of significance requires. They won't choose to push the gas pedal to get where they say they want to go.

I believe if asked, most people would say that they want more out of life, and that they are willing to make the choices necessary to obtain the life they desire. But once things get real, most often, you see people stop when they hit small roadblocks. Most people will even stop at mental roadblocks which are only real in their head. It's easy to recognize when other people are not living powerfully, but we all limit ourselves to some degree. Sadly, most people limit themselves far below their actual capacity. They may state that they have a goal, but fail to act upon the simplest and most basic of opportunities that could actually move them toward realizing success. You say you want a close relationship with a person, and then when they make attempts to spend time with you, you always make up an excuse. You say you want to be successful in your sales job, but then you refuse to pick up the phone, send an email, or otherwise reach out to interested potential customers. You say you want to lose weight, but won't stop eating doughnuts, and you refuse to go for a walk. You say you want to write a book, but you aren't typing any letters. Most people have impressive goals but won't even take a baby step toward that goal. Why is that? Why do most people seem to operate with unnecessary self-imposed limitations? And how do you break through those limitations to reach a place where you are consistently effective at achieving short and long-term goals?

LANGUAGE

Yes, I just made the word language as obnoxiously large as possible. The absolutely critical value, weight, and power of language cannot be overstated. Everything depends on your mastery of language, and the degree to which you master language will determine how well your life works. Beyond that, even your eternal salvation depends on language. Mastering language is a pre-requisite to mastering your free will, and to unlocking your full power to choose.

Duurp. Blleerrmmp. Donga duna flnia. Shssnkkltry. Jooshbedeety. Fananantrinithritygleenopop. Querteninty flonta zeeba doobie donona. Threninity flobagloobidyflop. Rendenendry nonapagroofity gunk. Gulgygoolgygulgygoogly nann. Sthroetheirityglhopppchipshhiienktyerlkjhsnitllksnnbkkthnlsidhhktklblishentklslkdihngkltkehl!

What in the world did I just type?? Nonsense. It was utter nonsense. I just typed random letters and tried to put them together in a way that still seemed like words, but that would be unidentifiable as any real language. I did this to begin to illustrate the significance and power (and sometimes lack thereof) of language. The letters typed in the paragraph above this one are worthless. They are meaningless. They create nothing of value outside of this illustration. They actually could begin to create confusion and chaos if someone tries to process them in their heads as meaningful, because they are not real words. Compare and contrast those worthless "words" I typed, against any real words. Real words communicate (transfer an idea, thought, process, or series of processes from one individual to another in a meaningful and impactful way). But it's bigger than that. Real words ARE power. Real words have the capacity to create. Real words also have the capacity to destroy. Words can be created by using some sort of tool to draw lines into shapes that become letters, which eventually become words. We can also use our mouth, our tongue, our vocal cords, our lungs, and the very breath of God that He breathed into us at creation, to create sounds which we have learned and agreed represent people, places, things, actions, realities, and thoughts. Both of these mechanisms, writing and speaking, are unique to those owning a spirit and soul (humans, angels, demons, and God). The trees cannot speak or write words. Animals, *(although some are able to create sounds, through which they have some basic level of ability to communicate)* do not have the ability to create words. Therefore, they lack the ability to create meaning, and they lack authority.

In the beginning was the Word and the Word was with God and the Word was God.

John 1:1

We all fail miserably to grasp the fullness of John 1:1. "In the beginning" means "principally" or "first". Before all of creation, and before time even existed, there was the Word. This means everything after that (every created thing) is subject to, created by, and lesser than, the Word. Everything after the Word must obey the Word. The Word is inherently perfect. The Word is inherently true. The Word is inherently holy. The Word is inherently the beginning and the end. The Word is inherently all powerful. The Word is inherently just. The Word is inherently order. The Word always was, is, and always will be God in every full sense.

Read Genesis 1. You will find the creation account is due to God <u>speaking</u>. Out loud. Over and over again we read, "God said", and "God called". Literally everything that is, is the result of God speaking words. He spoke all of creation into existence. He spoke order into being. Why is this important to our conversation about wellness?

And God said, Let us make man in our image, after our likeness: and let them have dominion over the fish of the sea, and over the fowl of the air, and over the cattle, and over all the earth, and over every creeping thing that creepeth upon the earth. So God created man in his own image, in the image of God created he him; male and female created he them.

Genesis 1:26-27

We are created in the image of God after His/ Their *(Father, Son, & Holy Spirit)* likeness. This is one of those two ditches on either side of the road conversations. Some people, even most Christians, will fall into the ditch of ignoring that we are made in the image of God and in His likeness, bearing some similarities, and gifted with some of His powers. These people have a form of godliness, but they deny the power thereof. They don't pick up their sword (the Word of God), they don't fight many battles, and they allow themselves to be pushed around by this evil world. They fall into the victim mentality, and allow themselves to be enslaved when their freedom has already been bought. They have the keys, but they don't turn on and drive the car, so they don't go anywhere. The people in the other ditch recognize this verse and then claim to have all of the power of God.

36

They even blaspheme and say that we are all God and all equal. This is false, a demonic lie, and a misinterpretation of scripture. An image is not the same as the original. If I take my driver's license and make a copy on my copy machine, I produce an image. The image bears some resemblances to the original and likenesses to the original, but it is not the original and, in some cases, lacks the authority of the original. This is one of the errors that Satan tries to use to lure people into some false religions, which we will cover later. He uses lies to lure people into his deception with their pride. Who doesn't want to be all powerful? Who doesn't want to be God? We all do on some level. Even the humblest among us, on some level, desire to be in full control, and desire to be the most High. The wicked condition of our flesh that came with the knowledge of good and evil is a constant desire to dominate and avoid being dominated. We see it everywhere, and in every interaction. If you look closely, most natural fleshly conversations are a calculated chess match where each person is attempting to dominate and avoid being dominated. Even if the insecurities and manipulations are tactful and subtle, they're normally still there. The only way that a conversation can be anything other than that, is when the words are anointed by the Holy Spirit to be life. Only a vessel which contains the Holy Spirit can speak words which are truly life, and 100% beneficial to others with no personal angle or ulterior motive. Only the Holy Spirit can love perfectly. Only the Word can speak life. Everything else is death, even if it is carefully concealed, packaged, and misrepresented as life. But I'm starting to digress. The point here, before we go deeper, is to acknowledge that we are made in the image of God and therefore we bear some of His likeness and power, but not all. We are not and will never be God, but we have, to a much lesser degree than He, a similar ability to create life with our words. This means that we also have a similar, but much lesser, ability as He to create death with our words.

Death and life are in the power of the tongue: and they that love it shall eat the fruit thereof.

Proverbs 18:21

It's longer so I'm not going to type it all out here, but go back and read Mark 11. Jesus cursed the fig tree and it withered up and died. Right after Peter noticed and pointed it out, Jesus' response was that "whosoever shall say unto this mountain, Be thou removed, and shall not doubt in his heart, but shall believe that those things which he saith shall come to pass; he shall have whatsoever he saith."

Seriously don't miss this. Jesus told us whosoever shall SAY, shall have. This is really specific. To get the full intended value out of this book, you will need to be able to understand the language being used. To create the greatest, fullest life that you can, you must master the understanding of language, and the writing and speaking of language. It is the highest and only true power that exists. Any endeavor with eternal fruit or eternal consequence will involve language. Any effort or activity which does not involve language is temporary and futile.

All words are power, but most words are limited by the set of constraints placed upon this world by our creator. One usually cannot simply speak words which break the architectural designs put in place and expect to see your words having authority. For example, if I say, "I command the wind to lift me in the air and fly me to the next town!" I'm probably going to be disappointed when I'm not moving anywhere.

And this is the confidence that we have in him, that, if we ask any thing according to his will, he heareth us:

1 John 5:14

There are plenty of instances where mankind was given authority over the created world that violated the natural order or rules that are normally in place. Joshua commanded the sun to stand still. Jesus commanded Lazarus to come forth. These words were only allowed to have authority to violate the natural order of the rules of this place, because in those specific instances, the words that were spoken were lined up in accordance to the will of God. They were anointed with His power and His will was done. This creates a difficult place for those made in His image. We desire to see the miraculous, but most people stop believing in the miraculous the first time that they say something and it doesn't happen in the physical. We are not always going to understand when our prayers seem to go unanswered and the miraculous seems to fail us. But there are those who choose to humble themselves and recognize that in their flesh they prayed something that, for some reason, was not the will of God and therefore was not anointed to break the normal rules of creation. They keep their faith that our God is the God of miracles, that He is the same yesterday, today, and forever, and that these things and greater shall we do in His name. They keep praying and believing, sometimes they do get to witness miracles, and their faith becomes stronger. The next time a miracle seems to escape, they don't lose faith and they don't become too discouraged. Maturity recognizes that a miracle is a miracle by definition, because it is not the norm.

Outside of speaking words that are intended to break the natural order of creation resulting in a miracle, there are a nearly limitless number of words that have power built in to the natural order of creation. Sadly, these truths are grossly misunderstood and greatly underappreciated. I hope to shed some light on these areas to empower you to speak "well" throughout the course of your regular life, and also to rise to the occasion as the Lord permits for you to speak the miraculous.

People begin to recognize limitation in the authority of their spoken words as a young person. You command your sibling to let go of a toy, and... they don't. We all began to explore our environments and began to understand the constraints placed upon us and our world early on. We learned over time where our words have power and authority, and where they didn't. The problem is, there are people who teach you incorrect limitations. As a young person, you are influenced by ignorant peers and elders, most of whom have also been influenced by the ignorant. This shows up very often in language which is limiting to a person. A family member may say to a young person, "nobody in our family has ever gone to college and you won't either". Then the young person grows up saying to themselves, "I won't go to college". And then unless new language is introduced, that person will not go to college. If that person is to go to college, at some point the language must shift from "I won't" or "I can't", to something like "I will", or "I can". Once that shift happens, eventually new language becomes a reality such as, "I am going to college", or "I am graduating next week", etc. Having people in your life who will speak words that lift you up and encourage you is truly an invaluable blessing. Having people in your life who speak death, destruction, and disease over you is a terrible curse and a major obstacle for many people to overcome if they desire a life of order, success, health, and wellness. Many people do overcome this obstacle, but it is not without words being spoken into their life which counteract the lies and speak truth. These words could come from a friend, neighbor, family member, teacher, coach, movie, book (ahem!), random person at the grocery store etc., but somewhere the good and helpful words were introduced. True words create life. True words break curses. True words reveal lies and take away their power. My goal in writing this book is to be one source of true words that will empower people, give them the tools to pursue a life of order/ wellness, and hopefully give them an encouraging push in that direction! My goal is also that at the end of this book, you will become empowered, and committed, to go out and to speak life and blessing into the lives of the people around you.

To say that the human brain has tremendous storage capacity is a gross understatement. A simple smell or sound as an adult can trigger a childhood memory that hasn't been remembered in 50 years. There are varying beliefs on exactly how much information is stored inside a person from their experiences. Some believe in a conscious and a subconscious, and that some data (thoughts and experiences) are buried deep and can only be brought out through meditation and counseling. I would caution all readers to stay away from psychotherapy. We are commanded in the Word to remain sober and alert (1 Peter 5:8). Allowing yourself to go into a meditative state where another person is in control is quite dangerous. I will go into more of those dangers in the I Am Spiritual chapter. But for the purposes of this conversation on language, I will simply state my belief that nearly all, if not all, of our experiences are stored and categorized in our brain. Some of them are operational in nature (how to walk, how to swallow food, etc.) Others are less critical, and of less perceived importance (lyrics to a song you heard years ago don't have much perceived relevance for survival/ success/ dominance/ avoiding being dominated in your daily life today), but they're all in there and they are all influencing your decision making, to some degree. They effectively create a pair of glasses through which you see, process, and experience the world. Some experiences are filed as having a greater weight or importance than others, and may influence you to a greater degree. Coming home to find your home burglarized as a young child may strongly impress upon you a sense of needing to be vigilant in securing your valuables as an adult. That experience may be thought about often and may produce strong feelings for many years. I'm sure you can think of many other examples of impactful experiences with varying levels of extremity. In the interest of dwelling on the excellent and praiseworthy I will limit my descriptions of the less desirable / more evil illustrations here to only those I think are necessary to get the point across. Since every thought and experience influences us and who we are, whether we are presently aware of them or not, the value of our experiences cannot be overstated. Quality experiences, and words which are rich in truth, peace, power, and love, sow those qualities into an individual and tend to produce more of that same fruit. Inversely, words and experiences which are consistent with hatred and chaos unfortunately tend to produce more of the same too. If there are some words that are consistent with life and order, and some other words which are consistent with death and chaos, it would behoove us to study them and understand them so that we can powerfully choose the language we are using, thus creating the life we want. This helps us, so that we can be careful to use the correct word for the intended purpose, and so that we are aware of the responsibility/ liability we incur when speaking. The more understanding we have regarding the power of the words that we speak, and how they affect others, the more we understand how accountable we are for the power that we create and release in the world through our words.

But I say unto you, That every idle word that men shall speak, they shall give account thereof in the day of judgement.

Matthew 12:36

Blessings and Curses

You can effectively organize all words into one of three categories: blessings, curses, & neutral words. Identifying the category a word falls into is fairly intuitive, so I won't try to list them, but the distinction between them is worth mentioning. Hopefully after reading this, you will be aware that many of your words do have tremendous power. Hopefully you will choose to use your words more carefully, such that your true intention for speaking is accomplished, and so that you only do good in speaking. Blessings are words, which when spoken, edify and strengthen, encourage and build, empower, lift up, and/or bring someone closer to God through truth, obedience, and intimacy. Blessings reduce or destroy the detrimental effects of evil in someone's life. Curses are words that decrease peace, separate us from truth and real love, weaken, harm, hurt, and bring chaos, suffering, and death. Neutral words are words which, when spoken, accomplish nothing by themselves, but are facilitators of either a blessing or a curse. They can be descriptive words, words that add clarity, etc. Blessings, curses, and neutral words can all be mixed together in a single sentence, which can be long or short. The longer and more complex a sentence becomes, the potential increases for there to be both blessings and curses present. You could dissect the language and figure out a weight or proportion. A sentence could be 50/50, or 20% blessing and 80% curse, etc. Our goal should be to speak 100% blessing to our family and the church. We should also usually speak blessings over our enemies, only speaking curses over them at the clear direction of the Holy Spirit. These instances would be the exception, not the rule. We are told in Luke 6:28 to "Bless those who curse you". But there are some instances, during heavy spiritual warfare, where the lives of the innocent are at stake, and the Father knows those persecuting us would not repent. He would sometimes rather carry away the souls of the evil than allow his innocent elect to be overcome. We will discuss that more later; for now, back to the power of words. Some words can go either way depending on the inflection or spirit behind the word being spoken. For example, have you ever walked into a business and been greeted with an authentic, enthusiastic, and joyful, "HELLO!" where you could genuinely feel that the person was happy to see you, and was being truly welcoming to you? Then, contrast that with someone who you maybe walked in front of at a grocery store, perhaps mistakenly cutting them off, and they respond with a, "HELLOOOOO!" filled with anger, resentment, bitterness, and maybe even a hatred that seems disproportionate for the offense? Of course, we all have interacted with thousands of people over our life and "get" (or understand) that the intention and emotion behind the word can change the meaning. Communication, then, can become quite complex. Not only do we need to say the right words in the right order, at the right time and at the right decibel level, but we need to check ourselves emotionally and spiritually (which we will discuss in their respective chapters) to make sure that we are communicating from a place of authentic love if we want to be a blessing in speaking. This is important not only in speaking toward others but also in speaking over yourself. Do you think it's a good idea to speak negative words out loud about yourself? Maybe if no one is around? The correct answer is a resounding, "no". It's never a good idea to speak negatively about yourself, even if you are joking, but especially if you are serious or your emotions are high. It is easy and natural to become discouraged when we mess up, fail, or have a moment where we drop the ball. It is quite common for people to curse themselves when this happens, unfortunately. So, when you drop your dinner plate and it smashes into a thousand pieces on the kitchen floor, and you waste all of the food you just worked so hard to prepare, rather than owning and acknowledging the mistake and moving on, like saying, "Wow that was really unfortunate. I need to be more careful next time", people will add unnecessary negative meaning to the event and then speak a curse over themselves and say something like, "I'm such an idiot, I can't do anything right, I hate my life!" and then that works them up, and before you know it, they have beaten the dog, drank a 1/5 of whiskey, and ran their car into a telephone pole. This downward spiral series of events was no accident. We will talk in later chapters about our terrible enemies, the evil spirits, the role they play in our challenges, and how to overcome them. But we start by only speaking what is so, and by speaking positively. It's fine to acknowledge the mistake. We're not living in a fantasy land or living in denial. The accident happened. It was costly. But *it* doesn't define you, unless *you* define yourself as such. "Wow, I dropped the plate. I can totally do better next time!", is a much better way to speak about the event, and sets you up for success next time around. It is almost always better to wait a moment, and to process the events transpiring around you before speaking. Taking a second to gather yourself, analyzing what's happening, coming up with a positive desirable outcome, and then choosing your words carefully such that they are consistent with achieving the desired outcome, will exponentially increase the likelihood of the desired outcome being the actual result. Speaking quickly out of impulse in response to an upset rarely creates anything excellent or praiseworthy. Nearly every time someone responds instantly to an upset, the response has come from the flesh which is partially hardwired, and partially conditioned to perpetuate destruction and chaos. In every moment, therefore, carefully choosing your words can mean the difference in creating a blessing or a curse for yourself.

Wherefore, my beloved brethren, let every man be swift to hear, slow to speak, slow to wrath

James 1:19

The accuracy of the words you use will be inconsistent without a mature understanding of the importance of "meaning" and how we go about assign meaning to words. Inherent in the design of language is the concept of meaning. Words derive their power from meaning. One word is different from another because of the meanings assigned to them. Meaning is understood by description and distinction. Description can be reading a definition in a book, listing attributes and qualities etc. Descriptions can be long or short. "Describe this apple"; "sweet". "Describe this apple"; "red". "Describe this apple", "crunchy". "Describe this apple", "soft" (could be the same apple but notice that crunchy and soft are relative terms that imply comparison to something else). With even the shortest description of a word, most people immediately form a firm opinion on its meaning and ignorantly assume to control a thorough understanding. This can lead to improper use and undesired outcomes. Some people are interested in learning, have a commitment to precision, and are willing to spend time seeking additional descriptions in order to gain a deeper and better understanding of the word's meaning. The greater one understands the true/ "truest" meaning of a word, the more powerfully they will be able to use the word, whether for good or evil, whether honestly or dishonestly. Distinction is also a very powerful tool for increasing one's understanding of meaning. Distinction is basically comparing two or more items or words to understand their similarities and differences. We are able to understand more deeply the true meaning of a thing or word when we understand how that thing or word compares to others. "This apple is crunchier than butter, but softer than a rock". If we have experience with butter, and experience with a rock, then we now have some context to understand what an apple is, even if we have never seen an apple. All of this is important because of the absolutely profound impact that the assignment of meaning has in our lives. We will talk more about meaning in greater detail in the I Am Emotional and I Am Social chapters, to gain tools for more powerfully pouring into those cups, but we couldn't breeze past meaning in a chapter on language and have that chapter retain its integrity. Take time to study language. Take time to master language. Mastering language will open up a world where nearly everything is possible. Mastering language will enable you to build the full life that your creator designed for you. Mastering language will help you to protect yourself from those who would use language to confuse and mislead you. Mastering language will help you to lead and serve others more effectively. The degree to which you master language will determine nearly everything in your life: the opportunities you create, the opportunities to which you are able to agree and participate, the traps you are able to avoid, the relationships you are able to create, the relationships you are able to maintain, the depth and intimacy of those relationships, the environment in which you will dwell, the amount of authority you will command in that environment, access to food, clothing, shelter, the quality of food, clothing, and shelter you control, your emotional state, the emotional state of those around you, the abundance or lack of time and cashflow, etc., we could really go on and on describing everything that depends on your mastery of language, but you should get the point by now. Everything, including all of the different components of wellness, depends on how well you hear, understand, speak, and otherwise communicate language. That's why we had to spend some time on language before we go into the details of how you fill each cup. I will use language in describing how to fill your wellness cups. You will process those words through the filters of the meanings you have currently in place. I will challenge you to be self-aware as you are reading this I Am Well series. Take a moment to notice how you feel as you are reading. If you find yourself becoming offended or irritated, pause and ask yourself "why am I really offended right now?" You may find that a word or words I use trigger some memory, that the offense is actually over some past experience, and not specifically what I said. This would indicate that you assigned a meaning of "offense", rather than a meaning of "contribution of goodwill" to the words I shared. It's true then, that just as you can also powerfully choose to associate the words I speak as negative, that you could also powerfully choose to associate the words I'm speaking as something positive. I hope that you will choose a positive association to my words. We will go through this process in greater detail in the I Am Emotional chapter, but there's a lot of meat between here and when we get there, so it warrants a moment here. Listen to your voice as you're reading. If you find yourself saying things like, "this guy doesn't know what he is talking about", you will find yourself receiving less value from the book. Much of what I will cover may take some time to fully understand and appreciate. Those who have the intellectual confidence in themselves to hang in there and get to the bottom of the point I may be trying to make, and who are willing to consider what I'm speaking, are much more likely to derive a benefit from their invested time than those who instantly shut down their listening when they hear or read something that may be new or contrary to a previous thought or belief they held. I promise that I will do my best to communicate as clearly as I can, within the confines of these pages, and I promise that my motivation behind taking this time is to add value to your earthly life, and to add value to your life in eternity. I hope you will continue to give me the honor of considering what I am taking the time to lay down for you in the coming pages.

So, begin taking control of your language. Begin speaking life and blessing over yourself and the people around you. Start by saying out loud,

"I'm going to get everything I can out of this book!"

"I will improve my understanding of wellness, and I will be well!"

The power of language and the spoken word is so important that, from here on out, I will begin and end every chapter with a prayer. My coaching for you to get the most from this book, is that you will benefit from actually reading those prayers out loud. Read and pray them from a place of sincerity and trust. Of course, feel free to add words to the prayers as the Holy Spirit leads. I'm not claiming that I will get everything right. But I'm fully persuaded, at least currently, that all of what I'm writing is true and helpful. And while I'm challenging you to read my prayers out loud, I will encourage you to speak your own prayers out loud too. Obviously, if the word tells us to pray without ceasing, then there will be times that those prayers will need to be silent prayers, but if we are taking the example of the One after whom we are created, He didn't <u>think</u> the world into existence, He <u>spoke</u> the world into existence. Perhaps the best thing you could actually do in life would be to read the entire Bible out loud. If you gain nothing else from this book but the practice of speaking holy prayers out loud, speaking positive blessings over yourself and your family, and NOT speaking curses or negative language about yourself out loud, then you will already have received immeasurable value. Obviously, I want you to stick around through the rest of the series because I think there is much, much more value available in the coming pages, but don't miss this first biggest nugget.

CHOOSE YOUR WORDS CAREFULLY AND INTENTIONALLY.

They are more powerful than you realize, and carry eternal significance and consequence for many people.

We just discussed how words receive their meaning from description and distinction. But description and distinction just help us to understand how words are different from one another and the specific impact that a word has. I've mentioned that words are also power, but where does that power actually come from?

AUTHORITY

I already mentioned that before time was the Word. All of His power has always been present. All authority is His. He is the absolute authority. He is the "author" after all!

All things were made by him; and without him was not any thing made that was made.

John 1:3

In his infinite wisdom, again with the interest of creating real love by allowing free will, He chose to delegate some of His authority to us. We were given dominion over the earth. We were given permission to speak. We were given permission to create life and death. We failed when we gave in to the temptation to eat of the tree of knowledge of good and evil and when we did that, we gave Satan much of the authority which God first gave us. Think about it all in terms of authority structures we see in place now. Those with greater levels of authority are able to move more in life with their words than those with lesser authority. The leaders of countries can literally kill millions of people with the single word spoken, "yes" or "no". I've heard it said that the sign someone has become truly powerful is that they spend most of their day simply saying "yes" and "no" to the questions presented by those under them. This is a really important concept to understand as we finish our conversation on language. The words that we speak have power, not because we are so powerful, but because God has delegated His authority to us. He has anointed us and appointed us to positions where we are supposed to carry forward and enact His will. May Your kingdom come, and may Your will be done on earth, as in Heaven. We are simply ambassadors in a foreign land right now doing the will of the King. If we abuse the authority given to us to speak into being something that is not the will of the King, there will be consequences. Again, every word we speak will be judged on judgement day as we read in Matthew 12:36. Every word spoken by every person has some power and authority in it. For example, a parent telling their child that they are stupid has much more weight in it than if that parent spoke those words to some other random child, because the parent actually has authority over their child. This is important of course to be careful with the words that we speak over those who are under our authority, but also brings to light the same caution we should have about the words being spoken to us and around us, especially by those in a position of any authority over us. We have to understand that we are not the only ones who have power in our words. Have you ever had an evil teacher or boss? Then you already have some understanding of where I'm going with this part of the authority conversation. A job can be miserable, simply because of the person who is in authority over you, and the words they speak. We will discuss more on the importance of powerfully choosing your environment and the people around you in the I Am Social and I Am Environmental chapters, but again there's always overlapping where concepts apply to multiple cups, so we have to address it here in the language section. Not only can we bless and curse those around us, but those around us can bless and curse us. I know most people, including most Christians, have believed the old childhood retort, "sticks and stones may break my bones, but words can never hurt me". This couldn't be further from the truth. Words actually do have the power to break bones and much worse. It's terribly unfortunate that most Christians are ignorant to this reality. The witches and Satanists sure believe in the power of words, and they use them relentlessly to torment those they hate, to usurp positions of power, to cause harm and death to their enemies, and to satisfy the orders of the demons controlling them. That's literally why it's called "spelling" when we articulate letters in an order that produces a word. We are effectively creating a spell that has power when we speak or write a word. This has a negative connotation to it which I understand, but that does not remove the truth that words have power when written and spoken. Our enemies understand this power intimately, while most Christians are willfully ignorant to this reality. We will talk about this more in the I Am Spiritual and I Am Social chapters, but for now let me at least introduce the terrible reality that if you are attempting to stand in any way, shape, or form for the kingdom of God and His righteousness, then you are on the radar of some evil people who are cursing you from the shadows with commitment to your total destruction. This is not to speak fear into your life, but rather to shine light in a dark place, and to expose the cowards and take away their power. Remember the conversation on authority. Greater is He that is in me than he that is in the world. Real Christians have the higher authority. We are more than conquerors through Christ who loved us. We will be victorious, IF we are aware that we are in a battle and IF we choose to fight. Sure, a rottweiler is way more powerful than a chihuahua, but if the rottweiler never fights back, even the chihuahua could eventually take the life of the much larger, much more powerful dog. And make no mistake, the kingdom of darkness has many highly trained assassins who almost always hide in the shadows where their victims are blind to their attacks. This is where their power comes from, darkness. Again, this is not to instill fear, but to bring a very real danger to your attention so you can be prepared and victorious. The enemy of our soul does not want us to be well. There was probably some spiritual warfare that went on before you even found this book in your hand. Sadly, I must warn you that there will probably be attacks as you read this book, and especially as you try to implement any of what I'm teaching. So, for example, if you start passing out and exhaustion tries to take you over every time you start reading, you may be under attack, and you will either continue to make slow progress and experience difficulty in retaining any of this information, OR you could choose to battle and say out loud,

"I BIND THESE SPIRITS OF EXHAUSTION, CONFUSION, AND SLUMBER IN JESUS' NAME,

AND I COMMAND THEM TO LOOSE ME IN JESUS' NAME!"

Then you still have the responsibility/ opportunity to use your will power to sit upright, turn on the lights, read earlier in the day when you still have some energy, put your phone to the side, etc. You can choose to do the things that are consistent with giving yourself the best chance for energy in the activity of studying/ reading. Again, I don't mean to keep kicking the can down the road and saying "we will cover this in greater detail in later chapters" but I am making notes of every promise I make to circle back, and will indeed hold up to my end of the deal if you hang in here with me. So, we will indeed discuss more on spiritual warfare in the I Am Spiritual chapter. We will indeed discuss more on effective study techniques for improving reading, and we will indeed go over exercises for increasing your ability to focus in the I Am Intellectual chapter. But, back to language and attacks you may face from language as you continue reading. Someone in your home may see you reading this and say something disparaging to you like, "What are you reading that for? You never finish reading a book". Or, "Wellness? Ha! You're the least healthy person I know". If words like these come up around you, simply rebuke them in Jesus' name and speak truth on top of them. You can even whisper under your breath, "Well I break that curse in Jesus' name and I WILL finish this book!'. Or, "I am improving my health and will continue to improve my wellness daily until the return of my Lord, in Jesus' name". Something. Just don't allow a curse to go unchallenged. Unchallenged curses are effectively received due to passivity and unexercised authority. Don't let the chihuahua eat you. Again, just be aware that there will be many challenges as you engage this book. Be vigilant and look for the roaring lion. Don't be passive. Be committed. Complete this, along with your other assignments.

We can't complete a chapter on language in a Christian book without addressing what is often an elephant in the room: Christians who use filthy language, i.e., speaking inappropriately, telling dirty jokes or using "cuss/curse words". I'm a man who grew up hearing lots of people using cuss words and telling dirty jokes. I have also been guilty of speaking this way. This type of language used to consume much of my conversations, (although I was at least smart enough to know when to speak differently around some people). Many of the people I spent time around not only excused this language, but celebrated and encouraged it. Looking back, those were some of the darkest years of my life. It's no surprise now, since I now understand the power of words and the power to bless or curse. There are many verses that address this, and it is important enough to list some of them here. These verses mean exactly what they say. Receive them as the specific and literal truth that they are. Going forward, conduct yourself wisely, and choose your words extremely carefully. Choose to powerfully and excellently articulately blessings. Choose to try to be holy.

Out of the same mouth proceedeth blessing and cursing. My brethren, these things ought not so to be.

James 3:10

Keep thy tongue from evil, and thy lips from speaking guile

Psalm 34:13

But now ye also put off all these; anger, wrath, malice, blasphemy, filthy communication out of your mouth.

Colossians 3:8

Let your speech be always with grace, seasoned with salt, that ye may know how ye ought to answer every man.

Colossians 4:6

Let no corrupt communication proceed out of your mouth, but that which is good to the use of edifying, that it may minister grace unto the hearers.

Ephesians 4:29

Neither filthiness, nor foolish talking, nor jesting, which are not convenient: but rather giving of thanks.

Ephesians 5:4

Not that which goeth into the mouth defileth a man; but that which cometh out of the mouth, this defileth a man.

Matthew 15:11

If any man among you seem to be religious, and bridleth not his tongue, but deceiveth his own heart, this man's religion is vain.

James 1:26

Let no man despise thy youth; but be thou an example of the believers, in word, in conversation, in charity, in spirit, in faith, in purity.

1 Timothy 4:12

But shun profane and vain babblings: for they will increase unto more ungodliness.

2 Timothy 2:16

His mouth is full of cursing and deceit and fraud: under his tongue is mischief and vanity.

Psalm 10:7
(In describing "the wicked")

Let the words of my mouth, and the meditation of my heart, be acceptable in thy sight, O LORD, my strength, and my redeemer.

Psalm 19:14

Put away from thee a froward mouth, and perverse lips put far from thee.

Proverbs 4:24

As he loved cursing, so let it come unto him: as he delighted not in blessing, so let it be far from him. As he clothed himself with cursing like as with his garment, so let it come into his bowels like water, and like oil into his bones.

Psalm 109:17-18

A naughty person, a wicked man, walketh with a froward mouth.

Proverbs 6:12

The fear of the LORD is to hate evil: pride, and arrogancy, and the evil way, and the froward mouth, do I hate.

Proverbs 8:13

The mouth of the just bringeth forth wisdom: but the froward tongue shall be cut out. The lips of the righteous know what is acceptable: but the mouth of the wicked speaketh frowardness.

Proverbs 10:31-32

The wicked is snared by the transgression of his lips: but the just shall come out of trouble.

Proverbs 12:13

Whoso keepeth his mouth and his tongue keepeth his soul from troubles.

Proverbs 21:23

Suffer not thy mouth to cause thy flesh to sin; neither say thou before the angel, that it was an error: wherefore should God be angry at thy voice, and destroy the work of thine hands?

Ecclesiastes 5:6

But I say unto you, That whosoever is angry with his brother without a cause shall be in danger of the judgment: and whosoever shall say to his brother, Raca, shall be in danger of the council: but whosoever shall say, Thou fool, shall be in danger of hell fire.

Matthew 5:22

For he that will love life, and see good days, let him refrain his tongue from evil, and his lips that they speak no guile

1 Peter 3:10

And there are many more that I could list but we have to move on. If you haven't gotten the point by now your heart is probably currently hardened in this area, and we may lose some readers by just sharing more and more verses. If you want more, simply search, "What does the Bible say about cursing" or "profanity" etc. This is bigger than most people realize and affects people terribly. It's not sufficient to just brush this off and say, "excuse my French" if someone that you think may be offended hears you cussing. Your words are power and have an impact in the real world, whether other physical ears are nearby or not. Stop cursing yourself and others. You are literally doing Satan's work for him. I've spoken to people who shared that they feel trapped in this language. They want to stop cursing and try not to, but find themselves speaking this way in spite of their desire to quit. Again, to truly gain victory over this cursing, we don't say "excuse my French". It's not the French language, and there is no "excusing it". Making an excuse for something allows it. We have to draw a harder line and take it more seriously. Saying, "sorry about my language" is at least a step toward repentance, but still lacks power and authority. If you are in the habit of cursing and want to stop, try a more direct approach. Pray a prayer about it out loud. Something like this:

"Father, please forgive me. I break that curse in Jesus' name. Cursing spirit, I bind you and I command you to loose me in Jesus' name! Leave me and never come back! I rebuke all unclean spirits and spirits of vulgarity in Jesus' name. I bless (this person/ this situation) in Jesus' name. Father may Your will be done here. Please wash me and make me clean and renew me. Please give me a clean heart and a clean tongue. Help me to be a blessing to others with my words. Father, please help me to do better. In Jesus' name, Amen."

You will likely need to pray a prayer similar to this frequently, and it may take some time to gain control over your tongue, but it is possible, and worth every bit of your effort and intentionality. Take control of your tongue and resist the urge to cuss. You won't regret it, and you may save yourself a significant amount of suffering and/or judgement down the road.

We've discussed how words can be a blessing or a curse, but there is value in understanding some additional categories under which these blessings and curses can fall. The first category I would like to discuss is blasphemy.

Blasphemy

Words have varying levels of power, authority, value, and impact. It makes sense then, that some words demand greater respect than others. It's also completely rational to understand that there is a direct relationship between your use of words, and the associated rewards or punishments that result. Using a word which commands great respect respectfully is appropriate and produces great blessing or reward. Inversely, using a word which commands great respect disrespectfully produces terrible curse and punishment. True justice and righteousness demand such. It would be difficult for us to perfectly rank every word in order of significance or importance, but there is no question that several words are at the very top of the list and demand the utmost of respect. There is some debate among believers as to the exact pronunciation of these words but the words that have the highest level of authority, and therefore demand the highest level of respect, are the names God has chosen for Himself. They all fall into three categories: Father, Son, & Holy Spirit. We won't go into great detail discussing the reality of the trinity where all three are simultaneously one and the same, but yet distinct from each other. That would derail us from our present focus on language. But I will address the trinity very briefly here to say that it is true that our creator, the holy uncreated one, is perfectly balanced as Father, Son, and Holy Spirit. He is perfectly available to us in relationship as all three, and as one. This mysterious reality is so perfect that in our flesh we will never fully understand this, or be able to articulate it. We are, however, able to experience this powerful truth in many ways along our journey. As we seek Him authentically and diligently, sometimes He rewards us with experiences of knowing. In a moment when He draws us near to Him, we feel His presence, sometimes in ways that are more powerful and intimate than any human interaction we could experience. In those moments, there is perfect peace in knowing He is who He says He is. Every word used to describe Him found in scripture in true. You know this is true with 100% certainty when you are in His presence. Just one such true interaction with Him will be enough to sustain your faith for a lifetime, and will help you face any trials before you with confidence that He is still in control. If you haven't experienced His presence in such a real and tangible way, then you need to diligently seek this by asking Him for it, and by being obedient when you are given some direction. He is a rewarder of those who diligently seek Him and make Him first. So do that. Above all else seek Him and His righteousness. Make obedience to Him your first and highest commitment, and He will bless you with an intimate understanding of who He is. He doesn't force Himself and His glory on us just yet, so most people, even Christians, never have these supernatural experiences because they take the whole relationship way too casually. How are you doing at honoring Him and His name(s)? The fear of the Lord is the beginning of wisdom. Do you truly fear Him? Do you truly respect and love His name and His word above everything? Do you treat His name and His word with the highest of respects? Or do you allow the world to manipulate you into cursing yourself by blaspheming His holy name? Blasphemy is any utterance of any words that fail to give your full admiration and respect to the LORD. We are all pitiful in our use of language in comparison to the Word, so there is no way we could accurately or adequately give Him the honor that He is due with our words. It's not about getting some magical combination of consonants and syllables just right, with the right accent. HE WANTS YOUR HEART. He wants all of it. Every single bit of your love and affection is due Him. If that is true for you, then He will speak through you and the words that you speak will be pleasing to Him. If He isn't truly your greatest passion and pleasure, then no attempt to give honor to His name with your language will ever be sufficient. But if your heart is truly His, then even the smallest of squeaks can be anointed, made holy, and can please Him and move mountains. I considered trying to draw out a chart with all of the names of God that we find in scripture. I considered touching on debates of timelines of letters in language here. I considered mentioning several of the big movements I see that are fighting for this pronunciation of His name or that pronunciation of His name. But I prayed about it, and have peace at least for the purpose of this chapter, that the heart issue I just mentioned is what is most important in pleasing God. I think with the history of deception this poor place we call earth has endured, that it's His great mercy that we are able to come to Him like a child and find His favor. Any good parent will understand this. The first time a baby makes a noise that is even remotely close to "dada" or "mama", or whatever you prefer, the parent is filled with joy and enthusiasm, and celebrates! Then as they grow and mature, the words they speak to get your attention and/ or to describe you change. Does this all of a sudden become an outrage? No, in fact if they are being obedient children, and you know that they love and respect you, they could call you just about anything and you would respond. We see a similar parallel in our own lives with friends, peers, and associates. Have any of you ever had a nickname? Did you respond to it? How do you feel if someone calls you a nickname, and you can tell they love you? It makes you feel good and you like them back, right? How do you feel if someone uses your formal real name, but they use it with disdain and disrespect? It displeases you right? So again, we see that the heart behind the utterance is in many ways more important than the utterance itself. And from an authority standpoint, consider any person in a position of power. Many times, once a person reaches a position of great influence, a pseudonym or alias of sorts arises. Some people even create alternate personifications under which to build a brand. I'm trying not to date myself and this writing too much by using specific examples, but Dwayne Johnson becomes "The Rock". Donald Trump simply becomes TRUMP. Your boss might have the nickname "Tiny". But if a co-worker comes to you and says, "Hey, Tiny wants this from you right away", that nickname would still carry authority and create a sense of urgency for you to move into action. The weight is not in the sounds of the name but in the authority which has been delegated to those sounds. The same leader could go by different names to different people, and the same authority could be distributed equally in fullness to each name. I've been in many positions of leadership and in many customer service roles. When I was in college my name was shortened to an abbreviated nickname, JMo. It was less formal than my full name, made me more approachable to my staff, and helped us to have a more personal and intimate relationship, but at the same time if JMo put you on the schedule, you still knew you needed to be there. They would also still respond if they heard, "Jonathan wants to talk to you about xyz", so it's not like sometimes going by "JMo" somehow voided out or diminished the authority I carried equally as "Jonathan". Most of us have at some time been called the wrong name entirely. If there was some well-meaning person who called you the wrong name, you probably weren't very offended, and depending on the circumstance you may not even have corrected them. I'm not suggesting that we can be flippant when we address our creator. I'm not suggesting that His name doesn't matter. I am trying to provide some context to illustrate the ditch on either side of the road here with blasphemy. On one side you have several different factions that will go so far as to say that you cannot even be saved if you don't pronounce His name in your best attempt at a Hebrew accent. On the other you have people that literally use His name as a curse word. I understand and appreciate a vehement interest in showing respect and honor to the name of the most High. I can also understand how some of these "sacred name" movements have gained traction. I can understand the rational argument behind trying to trace the history back to its most original source. I think there is also some value in looking at which name/ pronunciation/ combination of wind and vocal cord vibrations is presently hated more than all the others. Which name causes the wicked to get in an uproar? Which name is under attack more than any other, even and especially by the modern pharisee movement that claims to have some higher understanding?

JESUS.

You might have been able to confuse me into speaking Hebrew or searching through some dirty old scrolls for some hidden mysteries if I had not already experienced the miraculous by the spoken name of Jesus. I grew up in a pretty dead Southern Baptist church. There were lots of great people there who loved the Lord, but as a young person it was more informational than experiential (and unfortunately some of the information was wrong). I was baptized when I was 7 years old, but it wasn't until I was 14 years old at a summer Christian camp when I felt the hand of the LORD touch me for the first time. We were singing a song called, "Holy and Anointed One" by Vinyard Worship, and much of the song is simply singing His name as JESUS. It was during this song that I felt the hand of the LORD touch me. I felt His presence. I felt His goodness. I felt His sovereignty. I felt His love for me and His great power. I understood my wickedness perfectly. I knew that I really needed to be born again, and that my entire life needed to be for Him. I surrendered fully in that moment and wept in the beauty of His grace and mercy. After that I was never the same. Even when I later backslid and lived an intentionally sinful life (due to the security I thought I had from some false Calvinist teachings) I would still never forget that moment. It was and is an anchor for my faith that eventually brought me back into repentance and still encourages me to this day. That experience alone would have been enough to solidify for me that I will choose to worship and serve the name of Jesus above all others. But since then, there have been and continue to be many other experiences where the Lord blesses me and touches me and confirms for me when I am following His will, and I've been calling Him Jesus the whole time. There was a season when I had open vision into the spiritual realm. I could literally see demons as if they were in the flesh in front of me. As I studied and learned how to do spiritual warfare, it was at the name of JESUS that they would leave. I've seen people healed in the name of Jesus. I've experienced miracle healing myself IN THE NAME OF JESUS. I've prayed diligently over the years as different names are introduced by people as the name by which we are saved. My heart is sincerely to please Him. For years, I prayed that the Lord would forgive me and correct me if I was calling Him by a name that He found offensive, or to show me if He wanted me to call Him by a different name. I did not receive any specific word in either direction. It's not like the clouds instantly formed into letters or anything. But my soul finds rest in the name of Jesus. I sense love and experience power in the name of Jesus. I continue to pray to Jesus, and pray blessings and healing over people in the name of Jesus. And He still confirms for me on occasion that He is still with me and that I am following the course He has laid out for me closely enough that if I continue, I will indeed hear "well done". So, I know for me, I choose to call Him Jesus. I choose to worship Jesus. I rebuke demons and break curses in Jesus' name. I resist the devil in Jesus' name. I choose to read and believe Philippians 2:9-11 literally at face value in the English language that I understand.

> ***Wherefore God also hath highly exalted him, and given him a name which is above every name: That at the name of Jesus every knee should bow, of things in heaven, and things in earth, and things under the earth; And that every tongue should confess that Jesus Christ is Lord, to the glory of God the Father.***
>
> ***Philippians 2:9-11***

This does not mean that I think a Spanish-speaking person who pronounces Jesus "hay-soos" is in error. If they are seeking the Lord with their whole heart, I'm sure He answers their prayers and they are redeemed. Similarly, I believe it's possible that He finds it pleasing when some of His children call Him Yeshua, Yehoshua, Yahusha, or any of the variations we hear. Again, since I'm fully persuaded to use and call upon the name of Jesus, I'm not going to spend time trying to refute, counter, or confirm each and every "sacred name" iteration I've heard lately. Since the Lord has not spoken to me directly regarding the other names it would be presumptive and irresponsible for me to speak against them. I'm not going to risk blaspheming! I will, however, encourage you to test the spirits at play when people are discussing this topic. Is there a spirit of offense, bitterness, or pride present? Is there a lying spirit present? Is the Holy Spirit present? We could go down the same argumentative road with the name, "the Holy Spirit". Some people are saying that you have to identify the Holy Spirit by a specific name *(Ruak Kodesh or Ruak Ha'Kodesh is understood to be the correct pronunciation of the words originally used for "Holy Spirit" in Hebrew)* in order to commune with Him. I disagree. He is literally the only spirit which IS holy. All other spirits are unholy. So, by qualifying the spirit you seek as the "Holy Spirit", you have already disqualified all of the others. Again, if the Lord has spoken to you and revealed to you personally that it is His will for you to refer to the Father, the Son, or the Holy Spirit by a specific name, then far be it from me to speak against that. But you have zero chance in trying to get me to believe at this point that I am in disobedience by speaking the beautiful, precious name of Jesus or by listening to the Holy Spirit. I say let the fruit speak for itself. Take a look at the lives of those speaking different names, and see what sort of fruit they are producing. I've seen many convincing "teachers" on social media claiming that the name of Jesus is heresy, and this name or that name is holy. And then immediately they're also cussing, smoking cigars, and drinking alcohol. Some are morbidly obese, covered in demonic tattoos and piercings, and obviously lacking joy. I'm not condemning someone for smoking a cigar, having a drink, being overweight, or having tattoos or piercings, but I am pointing out the hypocrisy of someone who claims you are going to hell for eating bacon that defiles their temple in numerous other ways. To me, this hypocrisy causes doubt that their teachings are Holy Spirit inspired. So again, I encourage you to pray for wisdom and discernment regarding blasphemy. Commit yourself to avoiding blaspheming. Commit yourself truly to lifting up (presently, ongoing, and continuously) and exalting (presently, ongoing, and continuously) the name which is above every name. I trust that if you are sincere, you will be led according to His purpose for your life, and you will avoid this terrible offense.

Thou shalt not take the name of the LORD thy God in vain; for the LORD will not hold him guiltless that taketh his name in vain.

Exodus 20:7

And ye shall not swear by my name falsely, neither shalt thou profane the name of thy God: I am the LORD.

Leviticus 19:12

Thou shalt not take the name of the LORD thy God in vain: for the LORD will not hold him guiltless that taketh his name in vain.

Deuteronomy 5:11

He that is not with me is against me; and he that gathereth not with me scattereth abroad. Wherefore I say unto you, All manner of sin and blasphemy shall be forgiven unto men: but the blasphemy against the Holy Ghost shall not be forgiven unto men. And whosoever speaketh a word against the Son of man, it shall be forgiven him: but whosoever speaketh against the Holy Ghost, it shall not be forgiven him, neither in this world, neither in the world to come. Either make the tree good, and his fruit good; or else make the tree corrupt, and his fruit corrupt: for the tree is known by his fruit. O generation of vipers, how can ye, being evil, speak good things? for out of the abundance of the heart the mouth speaketh. A good man out of the good treasure of the heart bringeth forth good things: and an evil man out of the evil treasure bringeth forth evil things. But I say unto you, That every idle word that men shall speak, they shall give account thereof in the day of judgment. For by thy words thou shalt be justified, and by thy words thou shalt be condemned.

Matthew 12:30-37

But he that shall blaspheme against the Holy Ghost hath never forgiveness, but is in danger of eternal damnation.

Mark 3:29

In all things shewing thyself a pattern of good works: in doctrine shewing uncorruptness, gravity, sincerity, Sound speech, that cannot be condemned; that he that is of the contrary part may be ashamed, having no evil thing to say of you.

Titus 2:7-8

It shows respect and admiration to care about the name of the Lord, and to desire to please Him with the manner in which we address Him. When He returns however, at that last great and terrible day to slay the wicked and cleanse the world of all unrighteousness, He will have a name that no man knows. HalleluYah!

His eyes were as a flame of fire, and on his head were many crowns; and he had a name written, that no man knew, but he himself.

Revelation 19:12

Another category of language we should discuss are Oaths and Covenants.

Oaths and Covenants

If a man vow a vow unto the LORD, or swear an oath to bind his soul with a bond; he shall not break his word, he shall do according to all that proceedeth out of his mouth.

Numbers 30:2

They have spoken words, swearing falsely in making a covenant: thus judgment springeth up as hemlock in the furrows of the field.

Hosea 10:4

Again, ye have heard that it hath been said by them of old time, Thou shalt not forswear thyself, but shalt perform unto the Lord thine oaths: But I say unto you, Swear not at all; neither by heaven; for it is God's throne: Nor by the earth; for it is his footstool: neither by Jerusalem; for it is the city of the great King. Neither shalt thou swear by thy head, because thou canst not make one hair white or black. But let your communication be, Yea, yea; Nay, nay: for whatsoever is more than these cometh of evil.

Matthew 5:33-37

But above all things, my brethren, swear not, neither by heaven, neither by the earth, neither by any other oath: but let your yea be yea; and your nay, nay; lest ye fall into condemnation.

James 5:12

The scriptures are pretty straight forward here about taking oaths and making covenants. It's commonplace throughout the entire world in most cultures to take oaths and enter into covenants. So much so, that it is now impossible to live what would be considered a normal life without taking oaths and making covenants. To buy a house or a car you make a covenant. In order to legally become married, you enter into a covenant. In order to serve in the military or law enforcement, to practice medicine or hold public office, you must take an oath. These are all critical and honorable professions, and usually the oaths spoken seem to be good and righteous oaths. "Protect and Serve". "Do No Harm". Etc. In my flesh I applaud those who have taken these oaths upon themselves in sincerity. It's also possible that while they have the best of intentions, they have brought some level of curse upon themselves. We're told in scripture not to make oaths. I think there are probably varying levels of impact one takes upon themselves by making an oath or entering into a covenant. An oath taken with the sincere motivation of serving others selflessly is likely looked at differently by our Father than an oath taken with the selfish ambition to gain worldly influence and power. What I know to be true regarding oaths and covenants, is that if you make them, you better keep them. Many people make oaths and enter into covenants flippantly, not taking them seriously. They think they can just say whatever they need to say, to get the people around them to agree to, or do, whatever they are wanting in the moment, and then when it becomes inconvenient for them, they think they can simply violate the terms they entered into without consequence. This is never the case. There will always be a penalty imposed when an oath or covenant is broken. Sometimes the penalty is small, and sometimes the penalty is great. Penalties of broken oaths can sometimes affect the remainder of your life, the degree to which may vary. Sometimes that degree diminishes over time, and sometimes it increases over time. It is best to avoid making oaths as much as possible, because you never know how your environment or circumstances around you may change, and you may not have the ability to honor the oath. Sometimes people even enter into conflicting covenants and force themselves to be immediately out-of-integrity. This is very unwise and costly, even if you don't immediately perceive the loss. If you make an oath to someone and do not keep it, you may not perceive a penalty if the person doesn't punch you in the face, or sue you, or something. But then, you've damaged trust with that person. You may never even know the damage you caused to the relationship, or the true cost of that damage. Who knows, maybe even years later that person is in a position of authority that could be quite beneficial to you, but since trust is damaged you are unable to leverage the relationship for help in a critical moment. There is always a cost, whether you recognize it or not. So, let your "yes" be "yes", and let your "no" be "no". And be very sure of your answer, before you answer "yes" or "no"! Most of the time, there is great wisdom is taking time to thoroughly process a question or opportunity before giving a response, to make sure that you understand the question or opportunity fully, and that your answer is indeed how you wish to respond. The really big opportunities and questions warrant prayer and fasting to make sure that your response is not only what you wish, but that your answer is in agreement with God's specific will and direction for your life. Remember that there are varying levels of power to the agreements you make. Bailing on going for a walk with your neighbor carries less weight than standing before congress and being sworn into office. But your "yes" and your "no" effectively make small and large covenants every single time they are uttered. This introduces us to the very important concept of integrity. Integrity to me is simply doing what you say you are going to do, when you say you are going to do it. Something as small as being one minute late to a time you agreed to, places you outside-of-integrity on that one appointment. Most people will forgive that level of offense, but everyone has a different threshold for the amount of integrity they demand from those in their lives. You may be a person who has a really high tolerance for a lack of integrity. Maybe it really doesn't bother you that much

54

when someone doesn't keep their word. You may enjoy less stress than someone who is bothered highly by the lack of integrity they experience with others, but if you truly desire to have power in your language and to have influence in your environment, it would behoove you to strive to attain the highest level of personal integrity that you can. Just because you don't care if someone is late, doesn't mean that your next appointment will be as forgiving, and this brings us full circle to the penalty/ cost conversation we just had. If you are in the habit of disregarding commitments that your mouth has made with others, you are incurring costs whether you understand it or not. We will discuss more in the I Am Social chapter, but for now please just try to increase the level of importance and meaning that you assign to your own personal integrity. And not just in the words you speak and the covenants you make with others, but also with yourself! If you tell yourself, "I'm going to wake up at 7:00am, and I'm not going to snooze!", then you really need to do that. Nobody coerced you into making that commitment with yourself, and it's possible that nobody will know if you violate your integrity with yourself, but the cost is still great. Every single time you speak and deliver with integrity, the authority and power of your words increases; you push the snowball toward order. The same concept is true in the opposite direction; every single time you speak and fail to deliver, you are out-of-integrity, the authority of your words decreases, and you push the snowball toward chaos. Unfortunately, in this scenario your words have greater power. Remember that the plane we push the snowball on is tilted toward chaos, such that chaos decisions usually have a greater negative impact than the positive impact created from a similar level of order decisions. One way I remind myself of the importance of maintaining the highest level of integrity possible is with the slogan, "How you do anything is how you do everything". Of course, this is a generalization and not always necessarily strictly true in every situation, but the principle is biblical.

> **He that is faithful in that which is least is faithful also in much: and he that is unjust in the least is unjust also in much.**
>
> **Luke 16:10**

I've spoken to many people over the years who shared their great visions and goals with me, and their frustrations over the lack of progress toward the "greatness" they desire. Usually in these individuals there is (what I perceive) to be a very obvious lack of integrity, in one or many areas of their lives. I knew a guy at my gym who was a former pastor who had lost his church and talked often about how he really wanted to pastor again, and how he was waiting for God to provide and open doors. Then over time I noticed things like this individual frequently creating and leaving a massively terrible mess in the bathroom. He would leave weights laying around. He would leave sweaty clothes and personal belongings behind him almost every time he came to workout. I would often catch his eyes lusting after women in the club. I even received a fake business card, written in his handwriting, from a neighbor whom he had solicited, falsely claiming to be a personal trainer working for me. So, he was attempting to steal business from me and lied when I confronted him about it. And somehow through all of this, I did still sense an authentic love for the Lord and a desire to shepherd in the man. Somehow in his brain he was really not able to connect the dots to understand that he was not being faithful in the little things, and would therefore not be blessed with greater responsibility. Most people do this to some degree. They make excuses for themselves, and the weakness or wickedness of their flesh that causes them to fail to honor their word. This finally answers the question I posed right before I began speaking about language. How is it that people fail to achieve their declared short and long-term goals? How is it that they fail to effectively exercise the free will that God gave them? They lack integrity. They lack follow through.

They lack completion. How can they correct this? Simply begin to have integrity. It's such a simple concept, but somehow terribly difficult for most to accomplish. When you speak something, even when its small, and even when you think no one else will know, do (exercise your free will to move your body) what you said, regardless of the difficulty, inconvenience, or personal cost. Obviously in a complex, dynamic environment, you will have moments when, despite your best effort, you are unsuccessful and find yourself out-of-integrity. Sometimes the variables change, values, costs, and priorities change, and there are times when there is greater wisdom in letting go of something you spoke and allowing yourself to be out-of-integrity to a smaller concern, in order to be in-integrity with a larger more impactful concern. But those instances will be fewer and farther in between, if you exercise wisdom and caution before making commitments. The VAST majority of opportunities for integrity are well within your ability to honor. I would even go so far as to say that you "should" honor them. We will further discuss the impact of the word "should" and the weight and manipulative power of the word "should" in the I Am Social chapter. If we want to remove the guilt that comes with the word "should", I can simply rephrase my call for you to honor your word, and your integrity, by saying that honoring your word and maintaining your integrity is consistent with accomplishing your stated goals, and moves you closer to order and full wellness cups. You have the opportunity to choose. Just own the responsibility, the reality of your choices, and the degree to which you honor your word. A failure to honor your word is an inarguably clear statement you make to the world, that your level of commitment to any goals impacted by said choice is less than 100%. It's a lie to say you are fully committed to the achievement of a goal, when your choices are inconsistent with the achievement of the goal. It's not just a double-whammy, it's more like an octuple-whammy really. Not honoring your word not only places you in violation of a covenant, but also moves you further from achieving something that you do actually desire, lowers the respect that others have for you, decreases their trust in you, reduces the intimacy that is available with them, subtracts from future coordination and mutual benefit with them, and overall reduces the power that you have from which to operate. Your seemingly small decision to ignore the words that you spoke actually impacts every other area of your wellness to varying degrees. The more you get this, the more you will understand the weight and critical importance of not just every single word that you speak, but every single corresponding action that is required to maintain your integrity.

Stop undervaluing the words that you speak, the oaths you make, and the covenants you enter into. Assign the highest levels of meaning and importance toward maintaining impeccable integrity with as many people as possible. The degree to which you maintain your integrity will direct the course of your life, and determine the environments in which you will find yourself. The occupational opportunities which will be presented to you, and the responsibilities you will find yourself managing, depend on the integrity with which you managed prior covenants and tasks.

There is one more subsection of oaths and covenants we unfortunately must cover.

Deals with the Devil

Technically any agreement with the world that is in violation of God's Word is effectively a deal with the devil, since he is the temporary god of this world. I'm not talking about those agreements here. Those oaths and covenants will take care of themselves and end in their natural destruction. I'm talking here about the more intentional and sinister kind, the ones some people intentionally make with Satan himself.

We will discuss our enemy in greater detail in the next chapter, but as we've mentioned oaths and covenants here, I wanted to go ahead and touch on deals with the devil. There are people who knowingly enter into agreements with the devil. Some people reading this will begin to roll their eyes, and envision some person praying to some imaginary boogey man and writing a contract in their literal blood. I'm not debating that some wicked contracts are indeed signed in blood, but you need to understand that your words can be just as binding as a handwritten signature in your own blood. Unholy contracts can be signed or rejected with a simple "yes" or "no". When you enter into an unholy contract, a curse is created, but the opposite is true when comparing to a holy contract. If you uphold the terms of a holy covenant you are blessed, and if you do not uphold the terms of a holy contract, there is a penalty and could be a curse. As soon as you enter into an unholy contract you are already cursed, and the greater the degree to which you uphold the unholy contract, the greater your curse ultimately becomes. There is a lie in the church that all sins are the same. That's simply not true, and is not found anywhere in scripture. The verse they are taking out of context is:

For all have sinned, and come short of the glory of God

Romans 3:23

This is true, and clearly shows that every man and woman need the redemptive work of Jesus on the cross. We all need His precious blood to be redeemed and forgiven of sin. But this does not say that all sin is the same. God is righteous and perfect in the justice He administers. Do you really think stealing a paperclip from work is the same as murdering thousands of people? This is one of the many lies that has been sewn into the curriculum of most seminaries to cause doubt in people's hearts. How could a just God treat the two the same? He doesn't! In scripture we see that there are varying levels of punishment in hell, and that there are some sins which are "unto death" and some sins that are "not unto death". This is talking about the second death which is the fate of the soul, not the first death which is the death of the physical body.

If any man see his brother sin a sin which is not unto death, he shall ask, and he shall give him life for them that sin not unto death. There is a sin unto death: I do not say that he shall pray for it. All unrighteousness is sin: and there is a sin not unto death.

1 John 5:16-17

For if after they have escaped the pollutions of the world through the knowledge of the Lord and Saviour Jesus Christ, they are again entangled therein, and overcome, the latter end is worse with them than the beginning. For it had been better for them not to have known the way of righteousness, than, after they have known it, to turn from the holy commandment delivered unto them.

2 Peter 2: 20-21

We will discuss these truths in greater detail in the I Am Spiritual chapter. But for the purposes of the conversation on deals with the devil, first and foremost if you think that since you prayed a "prayer of salvation" at some point in your life that you are eternally secure, and somehow at liberty to make deals with the devil, you have believed a lie. If you are truly a Christian, you were bought at a great price and you cannot serve two masters. Don't think you can get away with trying to partake of all of the devil's delicacies and still somehow retain your citizenry in the kingdom of Heaven. Secondly, if you are a person who has entered into an unholy agreement (freemasons, witches, satanists, etc) and you now desire to break that contract, know that IT CAN BE DONE. The demons you thought you controlled will try to lie to you and tell you that you cannot escape, that God doesn't love you anymore and wouldn't take you back, etc. It's not true. If you are in an unholy covenant, and you still have any degree of regret about that agreement, that is a wonderful sign because it shows that God has not yet totally turned you over to a reprobate heart. If you continue in your wicked ways, eventually, any true light left in you will leave and you will no longer have any conviction or desire to turn away from your vomit. If you desire to break an unclean contract, I'm not going to promise that there won't still be some penalty for entering into it, but it can be broken, and you can be redeemed. Your life on earth may or may not be spared, but your eternal soul can absolutely be saved. You may or may not enter into the Lord's favor here on earth and be filled with joy and peace again on this side of eternity, but you can absolutely avoid spending time in the hands of the tormenters and eternity in the lake of fire. The only hope you have to accomplish this is the blood of Jesus, and the only way you can make claim to the power of His blood is to repent of your sins and commit everything that is your life to Jesus, regardless of the cost here on earth. If you do, the unholy contracts will be broken and you will enter into an infinitely more powerful contract with God Almighty. Then, He will do with you as He sees fit. Often though, those people who have repented from deals with the devil are protected here on earth and given mighty assignments, since they have access to people and places that your strait-laced Sunday school teacher doesn't. We will go into more detail on all of this in the I Am Spiritual chapter, but as we wrap up language and our discussion on oaths and covenants, I had to mention, your agreements with the devil can be marked invalid and unenforceable if you truly put your trust in Jesus. I know that there will be some people reading here to which this applies. I pray you will repent while you still can. Jesus is more powerful and He loves you. The grass truly is much, much greener on this side of the great chasm.

Praise, Worship, Prayer, and Tongues

We will go into greater depth on praise, worship, prayer, and tongues in the chapters devoted to the physical and spiritual components of wellness, but since we are still discussing language, we will briefly touch on the verbal contributions to these topics here. We discussed how terrible, detrimental, and damning blasphemy is to your relationship with God. Praise, worship, prayer, and tongues are on the complete opposite end of the spectrum. God loves it when we praise and worship Him! He loves it when we pray to Him! He loves it when we speak in tongues! The language used to participate in these actions always blesses us and blesses God. Again, we will go into greater detail later, but language used in praise recognizes and celebrates the greatness of God. Praise is kinda like a party you throw for God. Music can be involved, but is not necessarily required. You can even let out a shout of praise that isn't a specific word, but your heart is just exploding in excitement with a present acknowledgment of how great and magnificent and wonderful and good God is. Worship is a little different. Tons of people blur the two in their understanding and consider "praise & worship" to be a singular thing as if you are always doing both when you are doing one. If you look up the original Hebrew for the times that the words "praise" and "worship" are used in the Bible, you actually find that there were several different words with distinct meanings that were generalized in the translation to English. We will break them down in detail in the I Am Spiritual chapter. There are physical postures of worship too. Suffice it to say here though that the different types of praise and worship vary from excited celebrations of His goodness, to demonstrations of submission, to all out reverence and complete awe. I've heard that over 90% of the time the word "worship" translation is used, it is this "shachah" worship demonstrated by a prone position, on your face in complete surrender, completely overwhelmed and in awe of the awesome power of how holy He truly is. I haven't personally done a study on this with a calculator. But, from all of my experiences with God, and from what I understand about His nature, it meshes and makes sense that the form of worship He desires most from us would be the most reverent with the highest amount of submission. The greater one understands the depth of what "holy" means, the more in awe you become of who He is, the more you understand just how wicked and terrible you are have been, and how blessed you are that He is merciful. You understand with greater clarity the cost of your atonement through Jesus' sacrifice. Most Christians, even if they do consistently make any effort to participate in "praise and worship", truly spend most of their time aiming for the emotional high that can come with praise, rather than following the example of the Bible and spending most of their time in true worship, on their face in complete surrender, and in awe of the indescribable power and perfect goodness of the uncreated One who loves us and made a miraculous way for His miraculous creation to be redeemed to Him and restored in His glory. For them, it's more about the goosebumps they hope they will feel, than simply worshipping because of who He is, regardless of the "reward" the "worshipper" hopes to receive for "worshipping". So yes, there are spiritual and physical components of praise and worship that we will discuss at the appropriate times, but there is also a very important tie to language. Certain words bring us closer to true worship. Some words do their best in our feeble mankind attempt to ascribe true attributes to our King. Words like "holy". Words like "awesome", "terrible", "wonderful", "infinite", and many more that you can think of on your own. I think it is best to leave these words to be used exclusively in reverence for God in speaking to Him and in speaking about Him. We cheapen those words, and unfortunately weaken our already pathetic attempts to ascribe to Him the respect and honor due to Him, when we take the words that are reserved for Him and use them inappropriately. I'm sure that when we see this in culture there is a duality of efforts at play. Naming a dessert at a restaurant something like "divine chocolate cake", is a marketing effort to distinguish the dessert as a dessert that may have required more preparation and used higher quality ingredients, hopefully resulting in a more enjoyable dessert experience. Perhaps you are able to justify charging a little more, and to entice more people into ordering it. But, multiply the effect of that single instance of gross exaggeration times every other time in society that we see the word "divine" used to describe something other than God, and you really begin to cheapen the word. I think it's absolutely been a tactic of the devil to water down language used to describe God's glory. Somehow everything is "awesome". How are you doing today? "Awesome!". Really? Are you really so magnificent that others should be in awe of you? You see something mildly shocking or entertaining and exclaim, "Holy Cow!". Really? Was that video of a cat doing a backflip somehow on the same level as our perfect sinless savior? What does a cow have to do with it? You do know that the Hindu's regard cows as sacred right? Some will argue that using a statement such as "Holy Cow" is mocking Hinduism, and since Hinduism is a false religion that is ok. Really? You're still taking a word that should be reserved for the most

High and using it with disrespect. On some level you are even adding your agreement to the lie that a cow is holy, and giving that lie a degree of power in the world. If you were really self-aware, and operating with spiritual discernment, you would realize that a mocking spirit is present, and that it's not from God. I know that most people will think I'm making too big of a deal out of this. I'm not claiming to be perfect or to have transcended to some place where I only speak appropriately and accurately, somehow perfectly avoiding unintentional blasphemy, and somehow avoiding unintendedly glorifying created things. We've all been conditioned through society to speak this way. It happens on auto-pilot constantly. I however do make an effort to recognize these things, and pray that God would help me to change my language to be accurate, truly respectful, and powerful. I pray that the language I use would glorify only the one true God, the Lord Jesus. And when I recognize that I speak inappropriately, I try to own it and correct it, rather than leaving the poisonous seed to sit there. Speaking incorrectly brings curse and loss of power, into your life and the lives of everyone who hears them. So rather than ignoring it, I try to own up to it and correct it. And it doesn't have to be some terrible experience. For example, let's say one of my young children learns how to fold and fly a paper airplane and shows me in excitement, and my response is, "that's awesome!". I don't have to bring the moment down and make everyone feel bad and make a huge show out of my repentance and tear my shirt and start throwing ashes. I can still in a fun tone laugh and say something like, "well actually only God is truly awesome, but your airplane is the coolest thing I've seen in a long time! You totally made my day and I am proud of how smart and creative you are!" Put it in your own words, but rather than just leaving what was a pretty overused and uncreative response, I turn that around, give God glory, and speak a blessing over the child as they are left even happier than they were before. I will challenge you to be on the lookout for times when you speak inappropriately, or incorrectly speak words that should be used for praise or worship, and further challenge you to turn the situation into a blessing. There are tons of words we can use that are more accurate, that still allow us to have our own unique personality, and don't blaspheme or glorify something other than God. I believe that cumulatively, these improper word choices cause much more harm than we realize. When we begin to try to teach our children about who God is, we just lost a ton of descriptive power when we tell them "He is awesome", and they're like, "wait wasn't that cheeseburger you just ate awesome?" Same thing for adults. If you can get someone to church and the language there has lost some of its power because culture has depreciated its value through overuse and inappropriate assignment, you have a little bit of a harder time in your flesh trying to describe the indescribable. Obviously, the anointing of God will override that for a heart that is truly seeking, and can give them understanding that is supernatural, but you get my point. As much as you can, avoid contributing to the depreciation of words that should be reserved to describe God and His kingdom. You will one day give account for every idle or careless word you have ever spoken. For some, that is going to be quite a long and embarrassing segment of their judgement session before the throne. The other side of the conversation is also important. USE those beautiful words that describe our Father, and use them often, accurately! This means that you are spending more of your time speaking about the real glory of our King, distinguishing Him from everything else, and frequently pointing more people toward Him! Speaking about the glorious holiness of the only one who is truly holy is really the highest conversation you can have. Everything else is vain and eventually meaningless. We could, and hopefully will, spend an eternity discussing the holiness of our God, and we will spend more time doing this in the later chapters, so for now we need to move on, but one more time I will just say, choose your words and your descriptions of things more responsibly and accurately.

As with praise and worship, we will discuss prayer and tongues in later chapters too, but as usual, the overlap warrants a brief acknowledgement of them as they pertain to language. I've heard many pastors and lay people describe prayer as "just having a conversation with God". In one sense they are right. One distinction of prayer is that you are aiming your communication toward God. I understand the motivation behind that description is to encourage people to speak/pray to God more often. They hope to reduce the awkwardness that some feel when beginning praying. They hope to make God feel more approachable. They hope to help people develop a habit of praying more frequently. Hopefully, this will result in a deeper root system, greater surrender, truer repentance, greater obedience, and eventually eternal life. So, bravo, seriously! This is kind of a milk-fed understanding of prayer though, so if one never progresses and grows in their understanding of what prayer is, they will be in danger of having a form of godliness but denying the power thereof. Prayer is not just a conversation with one of our friends who happens to be the creator of all things. It's not on the same level. Prayer is a special conversation. It is the highest conversation since you are conversing with the most High. There really is true POWER in prayer. Most of the church has been misinformed that prayer is just us telling God what we want, and that He may or may not grant the request. As if you're away at college, and calling your parent at home who answers the phone, but then doesn't speak, and may or may not mail you the thing you asked for. Santa Claus, right? They are missing that we are made in God's image, and He has delegated His authority to those who are walking in true obedience to Him. He said He has given **us** the keys and that **we** will prevail over the gates of hell. God sets apart the time we commit to Him in prayer as special. There is a purification that takes place. There is an anointing that takes place. The prayers of true Christians are charged with a spiritual electricity if you want to call it that. Entities in the spiritual realm move when we pray, and these spiritual movements often create movements in the physical. Again, like I keep saying we will cover all of this in greater, more practical detail in later chapters but in our chapter on language here, pause just long enough to consider that prayer is not just a conversation with God. It is connection with God. It is the branch being connected to the vine. All life bringing truth and nutrients can flow everywhere they are needed, when the branch is connected. Ask God to help you in understanding the magnificent value of prayer. Ask God to call you into prayer more often. Ask God to give you a burning desire to connect with Him in prayer, and ask Him to help you to be found in obedience, actually praying when He calls you. Our battle is not against flesh and blood, so our enemy wants more than anything to keep people from praying. Nowadays, increasingly, if you want to do work and contribute to society, you have to connect to the internet. Let that feeble metaphor start to help you understanding how much more important it is to connect to your Heavenly Father. If you are not connecting often, and when you do connect, you are not spending much time before disconnecting, how much can you hope to accomplish? As with most things there is no substitution for time. Spend more time in prayer. The goal is to eventually "pray without ceasing". How much more vibrant, real, and active would your relationship with God be if you prayed earnestly without distraction for an entire hour, every single day? I promise that if you increase the time you are spending in prayer, you will begin to sense His presence more, even throughout the rest of the day. The more time you spend in prayer, the louder you hear His voice. The more time you spend in prayer, the more clarity, power, understanding, and meaning you find when reading the Bible. The more time you spend in prayer, the more assignments you will be given for the kingdom, and the more you will see the miraculous. You will see greater fruit created in your life, and in the lives of those around you. You will ultimately earn more honor and store up more treasures in Heaven. I believe the highest, most powerful form of prayer is speaking in tongues. There are many denominational arguments about speaking in tongues, and we will discuss the topic in greater detail later, but know that this book is written by a man who believes in tongues. There are different kinds of tongues: (1) one is speaking in a known tongue that the speaker does not understand but the audience does (like a person who normally only speaks English being able to miraculously speak Chinese to witness to a Chinese person), or (2) speaking in an unknown tongue (meaning speaking words that are not a language known to the speaker or anyone else). I believe both are biblical. I will lay out an abbreviated case for tongues later. But as we move closer to wrapping up the chapter on language, I'm mentioning it here because whether you think it's from God or not, you cannot argue that tongues is indeed a form of communication that creates. Even if you disagree that tongues today is from God, you must recognize, at least, that if you heard someone speaking in tongues it would make you feel a certain kind of way, so there is still some inherent power. If you disagree that speaking in tongues is, or at least can be legitimately from God today, I hope that you have enough confidence in your beliefs to continue engaging with the reading and challenging of the words in this book going forward. There is so much more value available in the other topics I will cover, that you would really be missing out if you tune out now. Seriously, please take a moment and reflect; process the words you are saying to yourself right now as the topic of tongues was brought up. Did you say something negative about me, or about other people you have heard mention this? Did you speak words, audibly or inaudibly that may have blasphemed the Holy Ghost, or cursed yourself, me, or someone else? Do you need to take a moment to repent and break that curse before we move forward? I come from the experience of being a Christian who did not speak in tongues for ~30 years. But then I heard some solid teachings and began to earnestly seek the Lord regarding this topic specifically, and eventually I became a Christian who not only believes one can speak in tongues, but became one who actually does speak in tongues, and knows with certainty by confirmation of the Holy Spirit that it is not only pleasing to our Father, but also tremendously beneficial for edifying or strengthening one's self, for power against the kingdom of darkness during intense spiritual warfare, and in supplication and interceding for others. If you are a Christian who has not yet been baptized by the Holy Ghost (as initially evidenced by the speaking of tongues), I implore you to hang in here with me and engage in the debate. Scrutinize what I will cover later, and take it to the Lord diligently. If there was a wonderful power and gift that God gave us to tear down the power of the principalities of darkness, wouldn't it be like Satan to attack the gift, distract from the gift, and confuse the church, if he was able, into not seeking or opening and receiving the gift? What if you were about to go off to war, and before you were leaving, somebody handed you a wrapped present and said, "this is the most powerful gun I can give you, and it will serve you well in war. Open it when you need it". And then you hopped in the car on the way to the airport with your Uber driver and the wrapped present, and he was like, "nah man there's no gun in there it's not going to help you, you should just go ahead and throw that away". Would you at least open the present and see if the gun was there?? That's all I'm asking and suggesting. Hang in here long enough for me to make the case for tongues and then take it before the Lord earnestly, and let Him show you whether it's legit or not. You might be expecting to find an empty box, and find out that you actually have access to a belt-fed, fully-automatic 50BMG with unlimited incendiary ammunition.

The Bible

Of course, in a chapter focusing on language in a Christian book, we're going to talk about the Bible. Whether you are a Christian or not, I really hope you will read this section. And whether you love, hate, or are indifferent toward the Bible, I hope you will press through and continue to read the rest of this I Am Well series to completion. If you allow this conversation on the Bible, for whatever reason, to derail you from completing this series, you will be missing out on much value. This may be one of those times where you are hearing voices trying to get you to put this book down, or to just skip this section. I challenge you to tell those voices to be silent in Jesus' name. Do it, even if you think it's silly. No matter where you stand in your faith, this section will probably be attacked more than any other to keep you from reading it. We will discuss the why and the who behind these attacks more in the coming chapters, but press through, fight, engage with, and focus on this section more than any other. Truly receiving the truth in this section will unlock everything else for you in the reading of this series, and really in every other one of your pursuits in life. One of my greatest goals in writing this book is to, in some way, or hopefully in many ways really, point you to the Bible and get you to read it as intentionally and often as possible, with the greatest levels of focus and faith as you can muster. The Bible is really the only source of truth. The Bible is really the only source of life. The Bible is really the only source of power. The Bible is really the only hope that exists. The Bible is the very Word of God. The Bible is The Word. Jesus is The Word made Flesh. So, in a sense, the Bible is Jesus. Are you letting Him get dusty on a shelf, or is He embarrassingly tucked away in a drawer somewhere? Seriously, you could just throw this book in the trash right now and go read your Bible and you would be better off. But since the Word is presently contained in the papers of a fragile little paper book, of course it is attacked relentlessly, and has been, since the first inspirations were etched in stone and written on papyrus. The Bible is attacked from every angle possible. This means you will see some attacks obviously out in the open. Many countries outright make possession of the Bible a crime punishable by imprisonment, torture, and/or death. This attack is quite obvious. Other more subtle attacks still occur though where the book is allowed legally. Sometimes it shows up in cartoons and tv shows by portraying someone who believes in the Bible as ignorant or even evil. Sometimes the attacks are as subtle as your Sunday school teacher or friend in small group, whispering a small admission that they doubt the entire book is true or to be taken literally. I will argue that the majority of the Bible (except where expressly stated to be metaphor, as in Jesus telling parables, or when prophesies are hidden in mystery) should be taken LITERALLY. Seriously, nearly the entire Bible should be read literally. If you go back and read the Bible literally, believing that it was written intentionally as literal, IT COMES ALIVE. Power is unlocked. Truth is unlocked. Deceptions are exposed. Curses are broken. Lives and souls are saved when you read it, and believe it, AS IT IS WRITTEN. Too many people who call themselves Christian's excuse away the majority of the book as poetry or allegory. The Bible is not just a helpful set of guidelines to living a peaceful life. It's not just some government mind control tool to keep us passive. I've heard these lies, and anyone who really reads the whole Bible will understand that the Bible is anything but a tool for controlling us and/or making us passive slaves to the government. The Bible is actually the only thing that will help/ encourage/ empower those in the end times to find the courage to resist the tyranny of the anti-Christ's one-world-beast-government system. The Bible is also not just a genie in a bottle where you can learn how to "live your best life", which most people understand to be gaining as many material possessions and the most influence possible. The Bible exposes us in our wickedness. The Bible cuts deep and calls us to repent. The Bible demands that we die to ourselves, meaning that we put 1st the kingdom of God and His righteousness above everything and anything else that we like or want. The Bible is literally living. Not to say that the words are changing or anything. The "Mandela Effect" is a lame lie from Satan designed to cause you to doubt the scriptures. No, the words written are not changing, but what I mean with "the Bible is living" is that the Lord can speak to you in an endless number of ways throughout the course of your life with it. One passage or set of passages may speak to you and edify you and encourage you or call you to repentance in one way, and the same scripture or set of scriptures may minister to you in a different way during a different season of life. It may be that your understanding has changed due to life experiences, or it may just be the Holy Spirit impressing upon you a different call for obedience, but the book is alive. Every time you pick it up, open it, and read it, you are connected directly with God Almighty. If you do so from a humble place of authentic surrender, and desire to know Him and please Him, He will be faithful to do some work in you. The more frequently and authentically you do so, He makes you more and more like Himself. Every person who calls themselves a Christian has some level of respect for the Word of God. Somehow, the weeds of life have a way of keeping even those who love and respect His Word the most from reading it, unfortunately. We should all endeavor to fight with tenacity to find consistent time with the Bible/ the Word. If you have a healthy relationship with your husband or wife, and there is a person who you knew hated you that was standing in your way of spending time with them, would you passively just accept that you were being prevented from spending time with the one you love? Or would you defend your relationship vehemently, and find a way to connect with the one you love? I am arguing that you should love your Bible more than you love your earthly spouse. Seriously, like infinitely more. Let your understanding of the passion you hold for your spouse (or the passion you imagine holding for a "perfect" spouse) be an example for the type of admiration and commitment you should hold toward your heavenly bridegroom. It may be hard for men to imagine being the bride of Christ, but if you pursue Him diligently, you will be happy to accept this title once you truly understand and experience His love. So, fight for your Bible. Fight for personal time with your Bible. Encourage your family to fight for their own personal time with their Bibles. Buy Bibles and give them to strangers. Know your Bible's different books and sections. Know where different stories are. Know how to find, even if it takes you some time, where scriptures are that will be helpful in evangelism. Know where to go to encourage yourself. Know where to go to find verses of encouragement for suffering brethren. Have some ability to defend the Bible's authenticity and inerrancy.

As a bible believing Christian, one objection I have heard many times throughout the years in opposition to accepting the Bible as the God-breathed, inspired, infallible Word of God Almighty Himself, is that the Bible was written by men. "How can you say that the Word of God is perfect when there are so many different translations? What makes you right and others wrong". Honestly, this is a very valid question, and one that leaves most Christians stumped, and either stuttering some ill-prepared and ineffective response, or resting on the crutch of faith. I'm glad that you have faith without seeing. You are justified because of that faith. Having some sort of justification for the validity of the Bible, however, will make you a more effective witness, and can only strengthen your faith even further. I personally have had so many intimate and powerful experiences, where God has touched me and revealed Himself to me, that I don't need any persuasion or apologetics to convince me of the validity of the Bible. But, in ministry school, I learned several points that can be helpful in evangelism if a non-believer is looking for historical and/or archaeological evidence/ validation. I won't go into tons of detail on them, because, again this book must be limited in scope or it would never end. But you can spend some time researching the following if you're interested in having more physical tools at your disposal to argue for the validity of the Bible. The following topics/ proofs/ talking points are more accepted as historically provable:

Masoretic Scribes

Take some time to look into the Masoretic scribes and the meticulous standards to which they committed themselves in copying manuscripts of the Old Testament. They had a specific type and quality of ink and parchment paper that had to be used. No individual letter could be written down without looking back at the copy in front of them. They counted all of the paragraphs, words, and even the letters so they could verify as they were going, by counting, if they had accomplished the transcription perfectly. They even knew the middle letter of each book so they could count back and see if they had missed anything.

Septuagint

Around 250BC the Hebrew scriptures were first translated into Greek. This was done by the order of the King of Egypt at the time, King Ptolemy II Philadelphus to put into the famous library in Alexandria. ~300 copies from 250BC still exist today.

Dead Sea Scrolls

Found in 1947, these manuscripts date back to 300BC and are in complete agreement with the next oldest group of manuscripts that we have from 1000AD. This proves that the Old Testament Bible we have today is the same as what we had in 300BC. This not only proves that great attention to detail helped to make sure they were the same, but also gives strength to the argument that the life of Jesus fulfilled Old Testament prophesy about the life, death, and resurrection of the Messiah (some liars will try to say that the prophesies were written after His life as propaganda). All books except for Ester were found, and there were only a few inconsistencies among them. These inconsistencies were only grammatical errors (punctuation, etc) but no content or meaning changes exist.

Archaeological Discoveries (Secular Sources)

- Sumerian tablets confirm the flood of Noah and list the different kingdoms described in the Bible. The Epic of Gilgamesh has details of the flood and Ark. This was written long before Moses was alive. The Sumerian tablets even record the confusion of language the occurred from the mess at the tower of babel.
- The Ebla tablets were discovered in the 1970's in northern Syria. These clay tablets dating back to 2300BC confirmed existence of Sodom and Gomorrah, Canaan, Potifer, and Ramsey.
- Merneptah Stele is a tablet found in 1896 and dating back to 1300BC which mentions Israel as a significant political entity.
- The Hittites were thought to be legend until their capital and records were dug up in Turkey.
- The walls of Jericho were discovered in the 1930's.
- The ruinous remains of Sodom and Gomorrah have been located southeast of the Dead Sea. Three feet thick buildings have been found burned, starting from the rooftops. At a fault line in the area, 95% pure sulfur balls have been found all over the area.

Some of those who try to run from Jesus try to say that there is no evidence that Jesus was even a real person. Madness. On top of all of the accounts of the apostles and writings of the New Testament, we also have writings from secular historians who were alive at the time that Jesus was alive. People don't argue about whether or not these people were real, and they acknowledged that Jesus was a real person (although sadly they didn't accept Him as Messiah, but at least this gives us secular sources from which to quote). Titus Flavius Josephus and Cornelius Tacitus are two of whom I am aware. Josephus is a widely regarded Jewish historian from the time. He was not a Christian and he recorded the Jewish-Roman war which resulted in the destruction of Jerusalem in 70AD. In "Josephus – The Antiquities of the Jews" he writes:

> "At this time there was a wise man called Jesus and his conduct was good, and he was known to be virtuous. Many people among the Jews and the other nations became his disciples. Pilate condemned him to be crucified and to die. But those who had become his disciples did not abandon his discipleship. They reported that he had appeared to them three days after his crucifixion and that he was alive. Accordingly, he was perhaps the Messiah, concerning whom the prophets have reported wonders. And the tribe of the Christians, so named after him, has not disappeared to this day."

Cornelis Tacitus was a Roman Senator and historian. In 115AD he wrote in "The Annals of Imperial Rome":

> "Consequently, to get rid of the report, Nero fastened the guilt and inflicted the most exquisite tortures on a class hated for their abominations, called Christians by the populace. Christus (or Christ) from whom the name had its origin, suffered the extreme penalty during the reign of Tiberius at the hands of one of our procurators, Pontius Pilate…"

As a side note here, I would like to point out that the term "Christian" originated during the time the church was born, shortly following the ascension of Jesus. I have known many people who proclaim to follow Jesus, who appear to sincerely love Him and follow Him, but who have rejected the title of "Christian" since so many atrocities have been committed by people claiming they are Christians. Wouldn't it be like an intelligent, strategic enemy to invest time giving true Christianity a bad reputation, by sending forth people pretending to be Christian who behaved otherwise? Sure, the term "Christian" has now become somewhat loaded, and for so many has a negative connotation. Rather than abandoning the label given to the early church fathers, the ones who walked with Him, learned from Him, loved Him, hugged Him, wept for Him, and suffered torture and death for Him as they proclaimed the gospel and launched the true church, I choose to embrace the label, and fight to expose those who wear the t-shirt falsely. I believe it honors all of the saints who came before us, who served, and died for His namesake and for His glory. I consider the ability to claim I'm in the real club as a great honor. I'm not mad at brethren who have been shamed or confused into rejecting this title and choosing to call themselves "Christ-followers" or something similar. I would just encourage you to be wary, because we know that in the end times there will be many false "Christs" who will present themselves and their false doctrines, and they will deceive many. So rather than going with "Child of the King" or some other title, I choose to go back as far as I can to when the real church first began, and boldly just embrace the term CHRISTIAN. Then when the hate flows, be prepared to defend your name badge. Sadly, it's not just the satanists who are against you. Over time the enemy has sown enough division, that the church is confused as to what to even call themselves. So, please consider not adding more confusion to an already lost world. Consider not sowing further division among the remnant. When you need law enforcement you call a Police

Officer. When you need a fire put out you call a Fire Fighter. If you are lost, feeling the call of God to repent, and want to be able to understand the Bible to learn how to seek Him and serve Him, knowing who you can go to who can legitimately help you, is invaluable. As it is now, most people are so confused, they think someone claiming to be some sort of spiritual guru, or some New-Age self-help promoting life coach is as qualified as a Christian in being able to help them with spiritual questions. Maybe we need to stop diluting the term "Christian" and stop dividing camps, and then more people would know who really has the information they seek? I hope the true church will continue to call themselves Christians until the glorious return of the Lord Jesus Christ of Nazareth.

And when he had found him, he brought him unto Antioch. And it came to pass, that a whole year they assembled themselves with the church, and taught much people.

And the disciples were called Christians first in Antioch.

Acts 11:26

Admittedly, historical and archaeological apologetics are not my forte, partially due I'm sure, to my confession earlier that the times where I have experienced God are more than rock-solid enough evidence for me to believe the Bible is true. I promise, if you ever really have an authentic encounter with the real God of the Bible, in that moment at least, you will <u>know</u> with certainty that every word He wrote about Himself in the Bible is true. After the moment passes, you are left in your flesh, and if you allow lying, deceiving spirits to influence you, it is of course possible that your faith could waiver, and you could begin to question again. But, if you stay vigilant about keeping "oil in your lamp" spiritually speaking by staying in prayer and reading God's Word consistently, your faith will remain high, and you will not question the authenticity of His Word again. That's another reason why I'm not investing tons more time in research to pad this section of the book much further. We could break down apologetics in more detail and discuss the Pilate Stone, The Burial Box of James the brother of Jesus, the discovery of the remains of Nazareth, Peter's house in Capernaum, the pool of Siloam, remains of Noah's Ark discovered in Turkey, the Shroud of Turin, evidence supporting the biblical account of creation, skeletal remains of the Nephilim, the hundreds of prophesies fulfilled by Jesus, and other physical evidences as large as the stars in the heavens or a small as DNA, but what I know is that no amount of physical evidence or proof will ever be enough to persuade the heart that is set on being hardened against God (although we will still touch on some of these topics later throughout this series). No effort at apologetics (which, why should we be "apologizing" in the first place) will convince those who are in love with this world that the Bible is legit. They won't care that there are over 24,000 original manuscript copies of the New Testament and that there are only 643 original copies of Homer's Iliad. Most people reading this are already firmly in one camp or another. Some people believe the Bible is perfectly holy and should be read literally. Some people think it's somehow holy on some level, but either contains errors or is not really to be taken literally. Some people think it is mostly just a book with some rules on how to treat each other nicely. Some think it's a government mind control tool to keep us subjective and passive. Some people even think worse things about the Bible that I refuse to acknowledge in writing. I'm not going to devote more time here and now specifically defending the Bible by pointing to physical evidence. I will however continue throughout the rest of this series to encourage you, wherever you sit or stand currently in your opinion of the Bible, to actually read it. Read it often. Read it daily. Read it out loud. Wherever you are, I hope you will begin to pray that God would help you to read the Bible, and to believe it. If you doubt its accuracy, or that its inspiration is divine, throw a prayer out there, even if you think the whole idea of prayer is silly, and ask God, sincerely, for even just one second, to reveal to you if the Bible is legit. Ask Him personally to reveal to you if the Bible should be trusted and read literally. Seriously, there is lots of useful information in the rest of this I Am Well series, and I do hope you will press through and read it to completion, but much of it is temporal and technically of little value compared to eternity. The most important and best thing you can do for yourself and the ones you love, which enables you to live a life where you are truly well, is to create of habit of consistently reading, studying, and meditating on the Bible. What I'm going to share next could help you to receive/ process/ understand more of the truth He has written for us to receive in the Bible.

You really need to be reading and studying the King James Version of the Bible.

No, not even the "New King James Version" … you need the real-deal, old-school KJV. I know, I know, most people can't stand trying to read the KJV Bible. With the way our culture has progressed, and the ways in which language has somewhat evolved, the King's old English really does seem like a foreign language to most present-day English-speaking people. And since it's more difficult and somewhat confusing, shouldn't we just use one of the more modern translations? No. Entertain me for just a moment. If the Bible is as important as I have tried to make it out to you, consider that the version may also be important. There are two main reasons I favor the KJV, and use it almost entirely. Before I get there, let me preface by saying I'm not technically a KJV only guy. I'm not one who is so hard core that I think you can't be saved by reading another version. I know that MANY people have been saved by reading and studying other versions. I'm not even going to go so far as many of my dear brothers and sisters who use the term "corrupted" when discussing the other versions. I think the other versions are still the Word of God and that God still uses them. I think it's even borderline blasphemous to refer to the altered versions as corrupted. But let me break down the debate and significance for you. Basically, the Old Testament was originally written in Hebrew and Aramaic. The New Testament was written in Greek. So, the people that argue that translating into English in the first place is a corruption of sorts have some level of standing, but I sure am thankful that both Testaments have been translated into English so I can read them in my native language! We just discussed the basic history of the Bible, and how scribes spent lots of time making sure they got everything right. Satan has hated the scriptures from the beginning, and has always tried to speak against the Word of God, every chance he has gotten. Many in the KJV only camp believe that a significant event (or series of events really) occurred in the war for truth, and the war to preserve God's Word. This was a dividing that created two different lineages of sources for translation. The two different sources are the Textus Receptus and the Alexandrian lines.

When you read through the book of Acts you find that as soon as the church was launching, Satan was on the offensive. He immediately began trying to infiltrate the church with false teachings. There were naturally some discussions that needed to take place for those converting Jews. They needed to understand the gospel, and the doctrines of the apostles that are the church's "constitution" if you want to call them that, which comprises the new contract/ covenant. Immediately, there was division in the church sown by those trying to hang on to Jewish tradition and the Mosaic laws. There were also efforts from Egyptian magicians to influence the formation of the church and teachings of the apostles. I believe the Textus Receptus line of text is the preserved, received from God line of text, and the Alexandrian text is the line that was influenced by Buddhists, Gnostics, and occultists. Remember that Satan is strategic. Yes, there is even a "Satanic Bible" written by Anton LaVey. This attack on, and insult to, God's Word is plain and obvious even for the most

68

lukewarm of Christians. It has its place in the arsenal of satanic weapons against humanity; it influences and encourages those who have already sold their soul in their conscious battle against God. But consider for a moment, if you really did have an enemy who was committed to your destruction, who was bound by certain rules of engagement, and usually only allowed to deceive you with lies rather than being allowed to physically attack you, would it be like him to find a way, for example, to manipulate a flight manual for your fighter jet? If so, would it be a useful tool against you if the manipulation was obvious to everyone? Not likely. If step one of the manual obviously had nothing to do with a fighter jet, the falsehood would be noticed immediately and discarded. No, a wiser more cunning plan would be to make the flight manual look very much like the original, accurate flight manual, and just weave some subtle differences into it. Perhaps the differences were even so subtle that unless you carefully studied both the original and the manipulated flight manual, line by line beside each other, you wouldn't be able to find the subtle differences. But what if your enemy was so cunning that the subtle differences still had a major impact? Like maybe you do indeed learn how to take off and land, but curiously, you can't find in the manual how to activate or use the weapons systems? You are up there in the air, engaging in warfare, but you have been somewhat disarmed so that you aren't as dangerous. Perhaps you have a cloaking device that helps you to avoid heat seeking missiles, but if you don't know where that button is, and how to use it, you are left more vulnerable. Perhaps a calculation presented to you in a formula used for navigation is 0.000001 degree off. At first when you begin your journey you are on the right track and seem to be headed in the right direction, but eventually that small error puts you off course and keeps you from reaching your destination. It's kind of like that with the Alexandrian text. Since the Bible is so large, and there are so many words there, to the casual reader they read pretty much the same, especially considering the difficulty most have with understanding old English. But what we now know from careful study is that while the Alexandrian text has most of the meat and potatoes of the real-deal gospel, there are thousands of "small" changes whose sum is quite significant. All of these changes reduce the perceived power of the gospel, and the perceived deity of Jesus Christ for the reader. This results in a form of godliness that denies the power thereof. It creates a weaker faith/ thinner armor. As we are still in our chapter on language, remember that words are power, and that our enemy has had several thousand years to perfect his craft of manipulating and deceiving us through language. On some level we all understand how susceptible we are to advertising through subtle marketing efforts. That's why companies will pay big money to have their product placed in the background on some popular tv show. They know if they stop the show you were so interested in for a commercial break, people would become aggravated and may even just walk away. But if the placement is so small and discreet that it doesn't take away from what the consumer is focused on, then the marketing impression is still made, and after the show, you are reaching for a specific bag of potato chips without even knowing why. It's like that with the Alexandrian text. In subtle ways our understanding of God's truth is undermined and we don't even realize it until some crazy guy in a book points it out. There are literally thousands of documented discrepancies that you can find if you begin to search. I won't try to record and review all of them here, but I will list a few to prove my point.

1 Timothy 3:16

1 Timothy 3:16 *King James Version (KJV)*

[16] And without controversy great is the mystery of godliness: **God** was manifest in the flesh, justified in the Spirit, seen of angels, preached unto the Gentiles, believed on in the world, received up into glory.

Versus

1 Timothy 3:16 *New International Version (NIV)*

16 Beyond all question, the mystery from which true godliness springs is great: **He** appeared in the flesh, was vindicated by the Spirit, was seen by angels, was preached among the nations, was believed on in the world, was taken up in glory.

Why is "He" used rather than "God"? Perhaps the translators had an interest in trying to convince people that Jesus was "just" the son of God, and not both the son of God and also God Himself simultaneously. It makes a really big difference. If Jesus was God Himself, His blood is even more powerful. If Jesus is God Himself, then God is not some distant entity that does not care about us or understand our suffering. Any good leader is willing to do what they ask from their team, or those over which they are in charge. It is an inaccurate viewpoint to view God's holiness as being unable to understand temptation. He came and endured pain, suffering, weakness, and temptation. He resisted sin, perfectly. Understanding that God came here personally, as Jesus, helps us to have a more intimate relationship with God the Father, and helps us to better understand the loving nature of God the Father. It's not that Jesus the Son is the nice one, and God the Father is the scary judge. Yes, there is an aspect of judgement within God the Father that we should fear, but there is also an aspect of perfect love within God the Father that we can cherish. There is also an aspect of judgement within Jesus the son that we should fear. This attempt to, in a subtle way, detract from the absolute deity of Jesus is a theme that is repeated in the "corrupted" versions over and over and over again in many different ways. This alone is enough for me to lean on KJV. But let's go through some more verses and look at a few more differences between versions.

Romans 14:10-12

Romans 14:10-12 *King James Version (KJV)*

10 But why dost thou judge thy brother? or why dost thou set at nought thy brother? for we shall all stand before the judgment seat of Christ.

11 For it is written, As I live, saith the Lord, every knee shall bow to me, and every tongue shall confess to God.

12 So then every one of us shall give account of himself to God.

Versus

Romans 14:10-12 *New International Version (NIV)*

10 You, then, why do you judge your brother or sister? Or why do you treat them with contempt? For we will all stand before God's judgment seat.

11 It is written: "'As surely as I live,' says the Lord, 'every knee will bow before me; every tongue will acknowledge God.'"

12 So then, each of us will give an account of ourselves to God.

Again, we see an attempt to create a separation between God and Christ. Why is the "judgement seat of Christ" changed to "God's judgment seat"? Could it be that many of these changes not only seek to decrease from the deity of Christ, but also seek to manipulate the readers' understanding of His personality and character? Sadly, most people today behave as if they believe that Jesus is just completely passive, timid, and weak. They think that Jesus only came to forgive, but they miss the fact that He is also our judge. They miss the fact that our words and actions will be judged, BY JESUS. He didn't just come here to give us a hug, a high five, and to tell us that we are "awesome" just like Him. He came and commanded us to repent, and expects that we will do our best to do just that. We will discuss the balance of being saved by grace through faith, and how that truth collides with our words and actions further in the I Am Spiritual chapter, so for now we will move on as we continue to make our case that KJV is the most reliable translation.

Acts 20:28

Acts 20:28 *King James Version (KJV)*

28 Take heed therefore unto yourselves, and to all the flock, over the which the Holy Ghost hath made you overseers, to feed the church of God, which he hath purchased with his own blood.

Versus

Acts 20:28 *New Revised Standard Version (NRSV)*

28 Keep watch over yourselves and over all the flock, of which the Holy Spirit has made you overseers, to shepherd the church of God that he obtained with the blood of his own Son.

Again, above we see a shameful effort to change the blood to be something less than God's own blood. It tries to somehow make the sacrifice less personal. No, I'm not trivializing the sacrifice of your one and only son. But the cost is even greater when the cost is both your one and only son, AND your own blood too! This change tries to diminish from the cost of the sacrifice, and also keeps trying to reduce Jesus to being less than God in the flesh once again.

Micah 5:2

Micah 5:2 *King James Version (KJV)*

2 But thou, Bethlehem Ephratah, though thou be little among the thousands of Judah, yet out of thee shall he come forth unto me that is to be ruler in Israel; whose goings forth have been from of old, **from everlasting**.

Versus

Micah 5:2 *New Revised Standard Version (NRSV)*

2 But you, O Bethlehem of Ephrathah, who are one of the little clans of Judah,
from you shall come forth for me one who is to rule in Israel, whose **origin** is from of old, from ancient days.

This one should make you angry. Here we see the translators blatantly change the text "from everlasting" to "whose origin is from old". Well, which one is it??? Is Jesus the Alpha and the Omega? Has He always been or does He have an origin? Saying that He has an "origin" incorrectly claims that there was a point in time that He was not and then eventually became.

Colossians 1:14

Colossians 1:14 *King James Version (KJV)*

¹⁴ In whom we have redemption **through his blood**, even the forgiveness of sins:

Versus

Colossians 1:14 *New Revised Standard Version (NRSV)*

¹⁴ in whom we have redemption, the forgiveness of sins.

What happened to the blood?!?! Was it just too many letters? Too hard to write a few more down? Or was there an interest in keeping people from thinking about the blood of Jesus? I take this one personally because of the following story: There was an instance once when I was fighting for my life as a result of a curse from someone practicing voodoo against me. I was about to go to the hospital because I thought I was dying. I was lying on the floor suddenly in inexplicable pain, crying out for mercy and begging the Lord for healing. I asked Him desperately to show me the source of the attack, and He showed me that voodoo and a person was behind it. (I will explain more of this story in the section on spiritual warfare). Immediately I repented for my passivity in allowing the attack and I cried out,

"I PLEAD THE BLOOD OF JESUS OVER MY BODY!!!"

Instantly, the terrible, excruciating pain I was feeling went away. I felt the Holy Spirit wash over me from the tip of my head down my entire body down to my toes, and I was instantly, miraculously healed. It was a beautiful and safe, very warm feeling that washed over me, covered me, and healed me. What would have happened if I had some lesser degree of faith in the blood of Jesus? What would have happened if I believed less in the power of the blood of Jesus, or worse yet, just didn't even think of the words "the blood of Jesus" because the words had been removed from the book I read, and were therefore effectively absent from my mind? Remember, the words that we think are the words that we see and hear in the world around us. If the Bible doesn't talk about the blood of Jesus, where else will we see or hear about it? The blood of Jesus is both physical and spiritual. The blood of Jesus is power. Why would a translator want to remove, or even risk removing, any degree of redemptive power from the Bible?

Zechariah 9:9

Zechariah 9:9 King James Version (KJV)

⁹ Rejoice greatly, O daughter of Zion; shout, O daughter of Jerusalem: behold, thy King cometh unto thee: **he is just, and having salvation**; lowly, and riding upon an ass, and upon a colt the foal of an ass.

Versus

Zechariah 9:9 New Revised Standard Version (NRSV)

⁹ Rejoice greatly, O daughter Zion! Shout aloud, O daughter Jerusalem! Lo, your king comes to you; triumphant and victorious is he, humble and riding on a donkey, on a colt, the foal of a donkey.

We will discuss false religions further in the I Am Spiritual chapter. One aspect they all have in common is that they deny that Jesus is the only way to heaven. We see that spirit was at work here in this translation. Why remove "he is just, and having salvation"? Well touching on a previous point, removing the "he is just" part makes him more like the easy-going hippie who is cool with everyone's sin. It also is an attempt to remove (Satan will take any degree, however small) the power of the truth that Jesus is coming back to judge. He will be a just judge and judgement will indeed occur. And the removing the "and having salvation" part takes away what should be another confirmation that Jesus is the way, the truth, and the life and that none come to the Father except through Him. Also, if there is this thing called salvation, then it implies there is a need to be saved from something. It's called our sinful wicked nature. Removing this salvation language from the text allows the reader to breeze past a reminder of our need for a savior, and hides who that one true savior actually is. Also, why did the NRSV feel the need to lower case the "k" in "king"? Some sort of low-key diss?

1 Peter 4:1

1 Peter 4:1 *King James Version (KJV)*

4 Forasmuch then as Christ hath **suffered for us** in the flesh, arm yourselves likewise with the same mind: for he that hath suffered in the flesh hath ceased from sin;

Versus

1 Peter 4:1 *New Revised Standard Version (NRSV)*

4 Since therefore Christ suffered in the flesh, arm yourselves also with the same intention (for whoever has suffered in the flesh has finished with sin),

Why did Christ suffer in the flesh? For us. "For us" gives the suffering meaning. When someone does something, and you know it was done specifically for you, you pay more attention. It is personal. You are more likely to appreciate what was done if you know it was done for you, and you are more likely to respond to the person who did it for you. This removal attempts to create some gap, a little wedge of distance, between the one who loves you more than anyone, and did more for you than anyone else ever will. The removal helps nothing and could potentially, to some degree, reduce the intimacy that is available between you and the one who suffered for you.

Mark 2:17

Mark 2:17 *King James Version (KJV)*

[17] When Jesus heard it, he saith unto them, They that are whole have no need of the physician, but they that are sick: I came not to call the righteous, but sinners **to repentance**.

Versus

Mark 2:17 *New American Standard Bible (NASB)*

[17] And hearing *this*, Jesus *said to them, "*It is* not those who are healthy who need a physician, but those who are sick; I did not come to call the righteous, but sinners."

Why did He call the sinners? Did He call them to come in for a hug? Did He call them to come play frisbee with Him? He called them "to repentance". I will go in greater detail in the I Am Spiritual chapter on the need/ commandment to repent and what that looks like. Entire denominations have unfortunately been built up that present a partial gospel. Removing the requirement to repent of your sins from the offer of salvation is one of the most creative deceptions of the devil, and one of the largest reasons that so many who thought they were saved will tragically hear "depart from me I never knew you". Seminary professors across many generations are guilty of teaching false doctrines of men in place of the simple gospel. Again, I will cover this in greater detail when the time arrives, but this is just one of many alterations in translation that aim to remove the word "repentance" from the mind of the reader. Shameful barely begins to describe this atrocity.

Luke 4:4

Luke 4:4 *King James Version (KJV)*

4 And Jesus answered him, saying, It is written, That man shall not live by bread alone,

but by every word of God.

Versus

Luke 4:4 *American Standard Version (ASV)*

4 And Jesus answered unto him, It is written, Man shall not live by bread alone.

Umm, that's partially helpful I suppose. Man shall not live by bread alone. Period? That's only half of the sentence and leaves out the solution! It leaves out what we actually live by! We live "BY EVERY WORD OF GOD". Many people who call themselves Christians do not really believe most of the Bible. If faith comes by hearing, and hearing the Word of God, is it logical to deduct that by hearing fewer words, we are receiving less faith? I think so. And the logic in this verse can be extended from faith to the context of life. If we live by EVERY Word of God, and we are receiving fewer words, do we have less life? I believe the terrible, truthful answer is yes. Less temporal life here, and for some, tragically, less life eternal. If people understood more how precious each and every word in the Bible truly is, would they prioritize reading it more? I believe many would. In fact, the amount of time and energy you invest reading and studying the Bible directly reflects the value you place on the words contained within.

Mark 16:9-20

Mark 16:9-20 King James Version (KJV)

9 Now when Jesus was risen early the first day of the week, he appeared first to Mary Magdalene, out of whom he had cast seven devils.

10 And she went and told them that had been with him, as they mourned and wept.

11 And they, when they had heard that he was alive, and had been seen of her, believed not.

12 After that he appeared in another form unto two of them, as they walked, and went into the country.

13 And they went and told it unto the residue: neither believed they them.

14 Afterward he appeared unto the eleven as they sat at meat, and upbraided them with their unbelief and hardness of heart, because they believed not them which had seen him after he was risen.

15 And he said unto them, Go ye into all the world, and preach the gospel to every creature.

16 He that believeth and is baptized shall be saved; but he that believeth not shall be damned.

17 And these signs shall follow them that believe; **In my name shall they cast out devils; they shall speak with new tongues;**

18 **They shall take up serpents; and if they drink any deadly thing, it shall not hurt them; they shall lay hands on the sick, and they shall recover.**

19 So then after the Lord had spoken unto them, he was received up into heaven, and sat on the right hand of God.

20 And they went forth, and preached every where, the Lord working with them, and confirming the word with signs following. Amen.

Versus

Well, there's nothing to even compare here because many translations have removed Mark 16:9-20 entirely! This is one of those moments where instructions for the weapons systems have been removed from the fighter jet user manual. So, you can fly, and be a vulnerable target while flying, but you have no ability to fight back. What activities/ actions made up the ministry of Jesus and His apostles? What did they spend their time doing? Yes, part of the time was spent teaching, preaching, prophesying, and calling people to repentance. Another massive chunk of their time was spent casting out demons and healing the sick! Most denominations don't acknowledge this. Of those that do, most say those ministry actions were only appropriate during those first few years of the church. Some don't necessarily speak against healing and casting out demons, but they simply refrain from ever attempting to participate in these actions. And people wonder why the church appears to be so powerless in today's culture. When someone is sick, do they go to the church elders to be prayed for? What level of faith would the "elders" even have if someone came to them? When a couple is struggling with their marriage, do they as Christians bind the spirits of lust and adultery that are tormenting them so, and command them to leave? Or do they seek counseling from some psychologist to try to "talk through things" like the rest of the world? If pastors and even regular every day Christians began to pray with faith for others to be healed, and it was commonplace to see demon spirits sent packing, what sort of testimony would that be to the unbelieving? What is the church really offering the secular world other than free coffee and a pat on the back? If Christians really had true faith for healing, would the world have been shut down over Covid-19? Would spirits of fear be consuming the world at an unprecedented rate? The answer is no. This removal of scripture bothers me more than most of the others, because it is a disarming of the saints. Many right-wing conservatives in the United States are adamant and vehement in the defense of their 2nd amendment right to keep and bear arms, and rightly so. But if our fight is not against flesh and bones, but against spiritual wickedness in high places, what are the real weapons of our warfare? How do we fight? Do we have any tools with which to fight, or are we just naked and vulnerable as the roaring lion prowls about looking for whom he may devour? Not only do we have some weapons available, but we are actually terribly mighty. So much so that we ARE victorious when we fight back in the spirit. But how victorious can someone be, even when they are truly mighty, if they have been convinced that they are weak and never told to stand up for themselves? Most Christians are like the big kid in the class who is getting bullied by everyone else because they won't stand up for themselves. Most Christians are the rottweiler who is being eaten alive by the chihuahua. This is why we see people struggling with the same sins over and over, generation after generation. We will discuss this in greater detail when we cover spiritual warfare later, but this one is so significant that it had to be addressed when discussing the alterations to the textus receptus. There are some theologians who will argue that Mark 16:9-20 was not part of the original text at all. I have heard that out of the 620 ancient manuscripts of Mark that have been found, 618 of them did indeed include these verses. I'm not interested in arguing that point. I didn't find the scrolls, I don't have personal knowledge of the Greek language, and I'm not personally able to argue that fact, or really any of the arguments about which lines were actually written on any pieces of paper. Really when it comes down to it, you are trusting that some "expert" person has figured out the truth before you when you are trying to memorize apologetical facts. And no matter how many facts you memorize, faith is ultimately never removed from the pursuit of God and real truth, so there will always be some retort from a hardened heart. In spite of this, however, I am completely persuaded that the words from Mark 16:9-20 are true because I have experienced deliverance from demons, miraculous healing, and the presence of the Holy Spirit. These experiences have been so powerful and extreme, that they are more real to me than most of the rest of existence that people are so willing to accept. I will continue to encourage true Christians to read Mark 16:9-20 as true, and to behave accordingly. Fight for yourself. Fight for your family. Fight for your brother and your neighbor. Your confidence, your faith, and your courage will increase with every victory.

I'm not going to spend more time here detailing the thousands of instances where there are differences between the King James Version and other versions. It's been done already and you can find entire books devoted to that understanding. I hope you have found this very brief introduction compelling enough to either just accept my encouragement to read and study KJV, or that your curiosity has been pricked enough that you will continue to study this out until you have unwavering confidence that the version you are reading is the most accurate version available to you. I pray that the version you are reading and studying is giving you the full context of the Word as it was intended to be given to us. I pray that the version you are reading is equipping you fully with the tools you need to be successful in being obedient to God, in seeing through all of the lies of the world, and in resisting the devil.

Another huge reason I like using the King James Version of the Bible for studying God's Word is the additional utility provided by "The Strong's Concordance". James Strong was a Theology Professor at the end of the 19th century who took the time to index every word in the Bible, and the corresponding original Greek and Hebrew words from which the KJV was translated. The importance of this tool cannot be over-emphasized. Of course, there is redemptive power just in the plain old English. You can just read the Bible in English and not only be saved but also have a very healthy and intimate relationship with Jesus. But we are told in 2 Timothy:

Study to shew thyself approved unto God, a workman that needeth not to be ashamed, rightly dividing the word of truth.

2 Timothy 2:15

I believe God wants us to continue to seek Him. He tells us that "deep calls to deep". We serve a God who always was, and always will be. That means there is an endless depth of knowledge, experience, and intimacy with Him that is available. It's beautiful really; those who enter into His courts will continue to grow closer and closer in relationship with Him for all of eternity. It's beyond mind-blowing to consider. So, while I won't have anything bad to say about someone who doesn't take much time to study the Hebrew and Greek if they are reading the English often, it's still true that we can find greater clarity when we study the original text. This greater clarity can reveal meaning and, oftentimes, strengthens one's faith. You can literally dissect (or divide) each and every word written in the English Bible to find out what the original word was. As big of a fan as I am of the KJV, there are still some limitations in the English language that made the translation problematic in a sense, because there are times when the English word used now typically is perceived to have a slightly different meaning than was originally intended. Taking time to study the words behind the words, helps to make sure we are not misinterpreting the Bible. There are many ways that this study can be tremendously valuable and important in your personal faith, and also in your evangelism efforts. Careful analysis of the original Hebrew and Greek tells a different creation story, it provides greater clarity on the history in the Bible and how the New Testament/ contract is different from the Old Testament/ contract. It simplifies and clarifies the gospel, and provides details which are helpful in understanding end time prophesy. I will break down some of these details as we work our way through this series. But in the meantime, let me challenge you to actually study the Bible. Don't just read it. If you are in the habit of just reading the Bible without studying it, you run the risk of filtering God's Word through your limited understanding, and then the potential for misunderstanding is great. By showing God that His Word is so important to you that you will sacrifice personal time in an effort to better understand Him so you can serve Him better, you position yourself as a candidate for blessing, and are in position to receive His wisdom and discernment. Don't be casual with His Word. It's not just a story to read while trying to remember a few helpful facts or life tips. The Bible is literally the interface and conduit between you and absolute truth. Diligent intentional connection to our creator through His written Word, and fervent prayer, are literally the only ways you can hope to receive real wisdom and supernatural discernment. The Strongs concordance, as well as the Thayers lexicon, are both very helpful tools in going deeper. I believe there is wisdom in keeping a hard copy of the Strongs laying around, just in case there is ever no electricity. But as long as we have access to technology, I will continue to use the Blue Letter Bible app on my phone. It is very fast and easy to use. It's a Bible app like most where you can search and find Bible verses. But all you have to do is touch on a word and navigate to the Interlinear/ Concordance tab and intense depth is made instantly available to you. The Blue Letter Bible app has aggregated information from Strongs and Thayers into a user-friendly tool. In a matter of seconds, you can have the full context of a Bible verse by analyzing the root words of a sentence one word at a time. Literally every word can be studied, and you will be surprised to say the least, at what you find when you begin to go into this type of study. You will be surprised to find areas where you were actually confused, and joyful in finding the deeper and clearer meanings. There are way too many examples for me to begin listing them here, but don't move on without praying and asking God if He would have you to study deeper. Make it a habit most of the time that you study or meditate on God's Word, to do a quick "background check", to make sure you are understanding everything correctly. I will go into some of the more impactful discoveries I have found as a result of studying the original text as we go through this I Am Well series. But don't limit yourself to the few I will share. Take this yoke upon yourself. You will be blown away at how the Bible explodes into life, and how real and profound your relationship with God (and understanding of His Word) becomes. I believe strongly (no pun intended) that a Christian who fails to spend time digging deeper into Gods Word by looking into the root words will always lack the highest levels of maturity in spirituality, faith, wisdom, courage, and character.

I believe one of the greatest and most significant areas of clarity you will find in studying the root words of the Bible is the understanding of verb tenses. In English, we understand a verb to be an action. "Running" is the physical action of moving your legs back and forth repeatedly, pushing yourself in a fast motion through space and time. In English how do we describe or distinguish between past, present, and future events? Sometimes we have a different word to use, and sometimes we have to add some words around the verb to qualify it. To describe the action of running which took place in the past we use the word "ran". To describe the act of running that is taking place currently we just say we "are running". To describe the act of running which will take place in the future we say something like, "we will run", or "we will be running". There really isn't a concise way to describe someone who is currently running who will never stop running, other than to just embrace a cumbersome sentence such as, "I am running currently and will continue to run forever". This limitation on our command of the language we are presently using creates confusion when trying to read and understand in full context the translations of the Bible. Here are the basic verb tenses we find in the original manuscripts:

- Aorist Tense – denotes an action that occurs at one point in time. Denotes the fact of an action and refers to the completion of the action without any reference to the length of the action
- Perfect Tense – indicates an action that happened in the past with results continuing in the present
- Present Tense – denotes linear action. Continuous, ongoing action, taking place in the present
- Future – denotes the contemplation or certain occurrence of an event which has not yet occurred

I'm going to stop right here to emphasize this point because this simple truth is incredibly profound and the misunderstanding of verb tenses has unfortunately opened the door for many false doctrines to infiltrate the church.

Do not miss this.

Many of the verbs we breeze past in our reading of the Bible are actually <u>present tense verbs</u>, meaning that the actions are taking place presently, <u>and</u> will continue taking place into the future.

This radically changes the true meaning of the text in many instances and has real impact on our faith as we walk with and seek after Jesus. For example, let's take a closer look at the first one that just came to mind:

Ask, and it shall be given you; seek, and ye shall find; knock, and it shall be opened unto you: For every one that asketh receiveth; and he that seeketh findeth; and to him that knocketh it shall be opened.

Matthew 7:7-8

Let's just go line by line, and verb by verb to break this down. The very first word is the first verb, "Ask".

- "Ask". This is a present tense verb. This does not mean ask one time and it shall be given to you. It means ask and keep asking. It's actually a deeper form of asking which can be interpreted as a form of continual begging backed by a real craving or deep and true desire. It's not a half-hearted ask, it's fully committed... so much so that you never stop asking and begging
- "shall be given": This is a future tense verb that is conditional on our present and ongoing "ask" or asking. So, if we authentically crave and beg continually, then at some point in the future it shall be given to us
- "seek": Present tense verb. And again, it's a deeper more meaningful form of seeking. It's a craving and actually a demanding of something from someone
- "ye shall find": Future tense. Again, this shows that if you crave and demand something from God, over and over again continuously, then eventually at some point in the future you will find it
- "knock": would you like to take a guess? Yep, present tense. You keep knocking. We "get" or understand this when we consider our own front door. If a solicitor knocks once and runs off, do we open the door and run after him and ask him what he wanted? For most people the answer is likely "no". But are you more likely to open the door and see what's up if someone is knocking and will not stop? Ok this could create a feeling of fear for some so instead of using the illustration of some grown man solicitor who has the ability to harm you, picture a small, precious, vulnerable child who won't stop banging on your door. Eventually you would ask them what they need, right? And if it's a good thing they actually need, you're probably going to do everything you can for them, right?
- "asketh": present tense
- "receiveth": present tense
- "seeketh": present tense
- "findeth": present tense
- "knocketh": present tense
- "it shall be opened": future tense

We see from a quick analysis of the verb tenses in these two verses that if we continuously ask and continuously seek and continuously knock, then we will continue to receive in part and we will continue to find in part, and if we continue this process then eventually at some point the door will be opened in full. Doesn't this provide a deeper level of detail? Does this inform the reader better on the true nature of the relationship and promise from the Father on how He interacts with and responds to us? Does it show us that there is a larger commitment of time and energy expense required on our side when we want something from Him? Would this be an encouragement to someone to keep seeking and to keep asking over time, and to not lose faith when they are not understanding something, or seeing a breakthrough for which they are praying? The inverse is true too, right? That if someone does not have an accurate understanding of the verb tenses here, and they read this and ask for something once and do not see their prayer answered, they could become discouraged and lose faith in these words, simply because their understanding of the verbs was incorrect?

Once we understand that there are multiple verb tenses behind the English verbs, and that a proper understanding of the verb tenses can change the true meaning, or at least give greater understanding of the depth of the meaning of a verse, then we see that these misunderstandings unfortunately abound and have terrible impact on the church/ body of Christ. Most preachers and teachers have failed to educate their flock on this very important distinction, and people are confused as a result! People are fighting through all of the spiritual warfare to try to get themselves in front of the Word of God, and then somehow the devil has found a way through language to leave a little pinky toe in the doorway, so a little confusion can sneak in and lead some people to chaos and destruction. I will break down some of the more impactful areas where verb tense has been overlooked as we work our way through this wellness book. But again, spend a little time to study the Bible. Understand the original meanings of the words you are reading, including the full depth of descriptions, distinctions, and verb tenses, and you will receive the full value that was intended, and is available. Do this on an ongoing, continuous manner, and you will receive the full value, continuously...

One point to note, is this is one place where the old English used in the King James is actually more helpful than our present English. Anywhere you see "eth" added to the end of a word, you can count on that verb being a present tense verb. But present tense verbs in King James are not always translated with an "eth". For example, above we saw both "Ask" and "asketh" used when the original verb tense was present. So, if you see a verb with "eth" behind it, you can simply process that in your brain, as you are reading, that it is present tense, easily, which is cool. But you should still look up the other verbs which omit "eth" as you study to clarify their tense, because they may also have been a present tense verb before translation.

As with every topic introduced in this book, we could continue talking about the Bible forever, but I have just a couple more points to share on the Bible and the KJV. We will discuss ways to stimulate your mind to make you "smarter" in the I Am Intellectual chapter. One way that we do this is by harnessing the electricity created in our brains to do things we currently perceive as being difficult. New motor unit pathways are created, and the new connections we create help us with everything we do. In this way, every experience we have, or skill we develop, helps us to some degree with other tasks which are perhaps perceived as not being related. For example, playing the old school video game Tetris, where you stack and organize different shapes as efficiently as possible, can help you to organize your room, or pack a moving truck better, later in life. Similarly, learning a new language just makes you smarter and helps you in many different ways in life. So, if reading KJV is difficult, good! This means you are growing and becoming smarter. On top of the benefits you are deriving from reading what I believe is the more accurate translation, you are also strengthening your brain which will serve you in many other ways as well. Boom, you just poured into your spiritual, physical, and intellectual cups simultaneously!

The last point I will make while I'm writing about the Bible here is just one more call to treat the Bible with the utmost respect, and highest level of fear and honor that you can muster. There are many who have cursed themselves by adding to or taking away from scripture. Father, please forgive me and correct me if I have ever done this. Readers, please meditate on the following scripture for a minute before moving on:

For I testify unto every man that heareth the words of the prophecy of this book, If any man shall add unto these things, God shall add unto him the plagues that are written in this book: And if any man shall take away from the words of the book of this prophecy, God shall take away his part out of the book of life, and out of the holy city, and from the things which are written in this book.

Revelation 22: 18-19

Selah

Selah means: pause and reflect

I know that for some (perhaps many) this chapter is getting kind of long. I'm going to try to "land the plane" here pretty soon. I hope you will forgive any perceived unnecessary belaboring of points. I am and will continue to do my best to balance being concise and thorough. I know we are still setting the framework for the wellness conversation, and many may be tempted to skip ahead to more of the tangible lists of do's and don'ts. I obviously think you should hang in here and read it in the order in which I am writing it. Lots of thought and intentionality is going into the introduction, the description of topics, and the building upon those topics in specific progression, so I hope you will powerfully choose to press through and focus as your interest in the words before you ebbs and flows. But there is abundant value throughout, so if you do find your fingers and eyes wandering about, I bless you, and I will just challenge you to commit to coming back at some point to the place where you left off, and to complete reading through this entire series in the authored sequence. Now for more on language:

Body Language

In addition to written and oral speaking, we also communicate with our bodies. The most obvious example is sign language. A person can literally learn to spell and communicate the same words that are able to be written or spoken, so sign language can be nearly as effective (I say only nearly as effective because the number of people who are able to understand sign language is much less than the number of people who can understand spoken language). A person who signs is even able to add to their speaking by adding to the signs with the rest of their body. When someone speaks words audibly, they are able to add excitement by speaking more loudly and/ or quickly. This communicates with greater detail, and has a different level of power once understood or received. You can also add excitement and power to sign language by signing more quickly, and using excited facial expressions. You are able to be very precise with sign language and communicate long, detailed thoughts. Sign language, while the most precise, is not the only form of communication that occurs with our bodies. We are constantly communicating with ourselves, with our environments, and with other people by moving our bodies. Every movement, from the largest down to the smallest, communicates. The best communicators will take time to become aware of their body movements. They will learn how other people, and even animals, typically assign meaning to body movements, and they will learn how to control their body movements to add power and impact to their communication efforts. Again, we see a correlation between the level of power and authority one commands, and the required level of exertion for an outcome. Those will little to no authority can do pretty much anything with their body and not much happens (picture a young poor child in a room or outside by themselves. What they do with their body doesn't create much for anyone other than themselves). But those with tremendous power and influence can cause much to happen with small physical movements. Picture the emperor giving a thumbs up, or a thumbs down, to signal whether or not the gladiator was given mercy and allowed to live. Or picture the President with his finger on top of a red nuclear weapon launch button. I know deploying nuclear warheads is not quite that simple, just go with me for the illustration. Greater leverage occurs with less effort as power increases. We will discuss more in the other chapters on how our body language affects ourselves, the people around us, and our environments, but it had to be mentioned here first in the language chapter. You are responsible for the communication of your body language, just as you are responsible for the words that you speak. Sometimes even more so. It's important to circle back to our conversation about meaning, and the creation and assignment of meaning here. Remember that people have the ability to create their own meaning, and it's possible that 100 different people could choose to create 100 different unique meanings from an identical event. It's possible then, for someone to be offended by your words or your body movements, even if you did not intend to offend them. The easier road to take, is to dominate and avoid being dominated by saying something like, "well that's their problem if they took it that way", and to a point you are right. It is quite the double standard to say that I have the power to choose my emotional response, and some sort of obligation to choose a positive response regardless of my initial natural signals, and then excuse the responses of others when they could have powerfully chosen a positive response themselves. Herein lies the burden of the advanced communicator. You don't really have to try to speak or communicate in a way that another person will receive well, but you have an opportunity to, and if you choose to take the yoke upon yourself and expend energy to communicate in a way that is a blessing to others, they may not even recognize or perceive the effort or the blessing. But God sees. He knows when you are putting others first and making any level of true sacrifice for the benefit of another. When you do take the time to communicate, specifically with the benefit of others as your intention, wonderful and great opportunities and experiences are created. I see tons of people taking the easier road of not caring about the emotional wellbeing of others, under the guise of "keeping it real" or some other façade. Really, they're just being emotionally immature, selfish, lazy, and displaying their poor communication ability and lack of compassion for the world to see. And people do see it. Whether the short-sighted, poor communicator realizes it or not, people pick up on all the little communications, however subtle, both verbal and non-verbal. What you put out there with your communication is creating your environment, to no small degree. Part of this is unavoidable. If you are authentically really selfish and hate everyone around you, it's going to be really hard to pretend that you like them, and actually convince them so. But even if someone can tell you are faking it, faking it is usually appreciated to some degree, more than outright blatant disrespect. Here is a small example: Often in customer service environments, I've noticed a worker putting a smile on their face in front of a customer. You can usually tell with a fair amount of accuracy whether that smile is authentic, if the smile is faked because the person has something going on personally that has nothing to do with you, or if the person is faking the smile because they have a problem specifically with you. The customer usually appreciates the authentic smile the most, but will have compassion on the worker who is faking due to unrelated issues. You can even tell the difference between a person who is faking a smile who hates your guts, but still wants to serve you and get through the interaction, from the person who is smiling at you in a passive aggressive attempt to instigate an altercation. Part of all of this sensitivity is just spiritual discernment and knowing the spirits that are at play. But part of it is learned culturally, and is at risk of misinterpretation. In all of the cases above, whatever level of benefit or appreciation was created from the workers effort to smile, is greatly depreciated when that smile instantly vanishes as the person turns away. I can't tell you how many times I've watched big smiles melt one microsecond after the person thought they were able to stop their effort. What most people fail to realize is that people are always watching… all the time. So, either go through with the full effort to fake it until you make it, and just keep that fake smile on through your entire shift (or at least every single time it's even remotely possible for a customer to see you), or don't, because you lose all relational currency and even go into the negative once people realize you are being fake. I've watched waiters roll their eyes walking away from one table, and then walk up to me with the same fake smile I just watched them use with the previous table. They really weren't aware of their environment enough to realize that they are on display, and their true heart was just exposed. This verse comes to mind:

O generation of vipers, how can ye, being evil, speak good things? for out of the abundance of the heart the mouth speaketh.

Matthew 12:34

Out of the abundance of the heart the mouth speaketh, and I would go so far as to say out of the abundance of the heart the body moveth! If we keep going with the waiter illustration, what communication takes place when your waiter slams down the napkins you asked for, and walks away without making eye contact? What does it communicate if they place them down gently, away from your toddler showing that they put some thought into reducing a potential future stress for you, kindly wait until you make eye contact and genuinely ask if there is anything else they can do for you? I may just have to write an entire book on body language at some point, because it's so powerful and there is so much to mastering it. We will go into some greater detail later, but for now, we have integrity with our language chapter and this introduction of body language. With, oral, written, and body language, it's always going to be easier to communicate goodness, love, and kindness, if that is truly who you are. You may be able to fake it with some people for a while, but eventually everyone will figure you out. If you are one of those people who genuinely desires a shift in who you are authentically as a person, we will walk through some very effective techniques for creating the person you want to be as we go through this series. We will discuss how to make physical changes to your body in the I Am Physical chapter. If you want to become "smarter" we will go through ways to tap into more of your intelligence in the I Am Intellectual chapter. And likewise, if you are wanting to become someone who genuinely loves people, wants the best for them, and wants to serve them, we will discuss how to become that person in the I Am Emotional and I Am Social chapters. It requires some effort to create change, and it requires even more effort to create transformation, but you really do have the ability (to a very large degree) to create who you are, and how you authentically act and react. We're not quite yet there though.

The Intersection of Free Will, Language, and Your Wellness Cups

We've invested a fair amount of time, focus, and intentionality in our discussion so far, describing and distinguishing free will and language. I'll emphasize that there is much more to this discussion which has been omitted, partly due to time, space, probable focus limitations, and my own immaturity and ignorance. I will continue to seek a greater depth of understanding and control of my own free will. I will also continue to seek greater understanding of the power of language, and will seek to increase my command of this beautiful/ terrible responsibility. I hope that you will choose the same. It will be helpful to encourage our readers here to carry that torch/ burden/ blessing by explaining with just a little more detail, the eternal significance of free will and our words. Since we are going on this exploration of wellness here together, we will wrap up this chapter by clarifying just a bit further how free will and language help us/ facilitate the filling of each wellness component's cup.

We've spent so much time here discussing words, language, and free will, not just because they have power and significance, and help us fill up our wellness cups, but because some words and some actions have ETERNAL power, significance, and consequence. Don't finish this chapter without understanding the full weight of this responsibility. If you acknowledge Jesus with your lips before men, He will acknowledge you before His Father in heaven. We will give account for every word we spoke here, when we stand before God Almighty to be judged. Will your words testify that you believed on Jesus? Did you share His truth and His gospel with anyone? Did you have the opportunity and ability to save someone, and if you did have an opportunity, did you act and speak? Once you understand that every gift you have is from God, you understand that your time is not really your time, and your money is not really your money. Your energy is not really even your energy. Did you use that time and talent according to the master's wishes? The parable of the talents frightens me and lights a fire under me more than all of the others. If you are not familiar with this parable please stop right now and go read Matthew 25:14-30. I know that I'm not the servant who was trusted with just one talent (and if you are able to read and comprehend this book then neither are you). So, there will be much that is expected of me, and much that is expected of you, when we are judged. It's not just enough to acknowledge who the master is; He is expecting a return on His investment. We are bound by time and there are only so many minutes in each day, so you are literally spending the Lord's currency with each passing second. Even your sleep has a cost. Each word you speak is an investment of His currency. Each action you take, and movement you make, is an investment of His currency. Once you gain an understanding of the magnitude of importance a single decision can have on multiple areas of wellness, and on eternity for yourself and everyone you remotely impact, you begin to understand the weight of each decision, and the weight of the accumulation of your decisions. It is wise and helpful then, to carefully consider as many decisions as can be practically considered, through the following process:

Pray, ask God, and then ask yourself:

- What is the will of my Heavenly Father here? What pleases Him?
- Which areas of my personal wellness are improved by this decision, and by how much/ to what extent?
- What positive impact will this decision have on the lives of others in which I have influence?
- Which areas of my personal wellness are negatively affected by this decision, and by how much/ to what extent?

84

- What negative impact will this decision have on the lives of others in which I have influence?
- What will be the balance/ net effect on my entire wellness tray (all of my cups)?
- What will be the balance/ net effect on the entire wellness trays of the people for which I am responsible, or with whom I have influence?
- Which words do I/ can it/ should I use to accomplish the stated objective here?
- What power am I really releasing here with my words?
- Which actions do I/ can I/ should I take, if I want to be in-integrity with my stated goals?
- Which actions are consistent with my stated commitments?
- Am I willing to expend the mental, physical, and spiritual energy to speak these words and take these actions, all the way through to their completion?
- Am I willing to live with the result(s) of my action(s) or inaction(s)?
- What is my choice?
- CHOOSE
- ACT

This is basically just a more focused and thorough cost/ benefit analysis which understands the fuller extent of the impact of a decision, considering all of the many areas of your life, and the lives of others that the decision impacts. Most people do this on some level. My goal in writing this series, is to educate you on the different wellness cups and the interactions and dependencies between them, so you are making more informed decisions, and choosing to relate to this process with greater ownership. Obviously, with some decisions, you will have more time, and with others you will have less time to go through the decision weight-analysis process above. I believe the extent to which you are thorough in your decision-making and action-execution processes directly determines the quality of the results of your choice. For some people, simply stopping and asking, "wait, should I really do this?", would be an upgrade. Where ever you find yourself in your ability to understand and follow the process outlined above, aim to INCREASE YOUR INTENTIONALITY around making sound wellness decisions. Try to begin considering how your choice affects more than one "cup", and eventually, try to consider how your choice will affect *all* of your cups. Commit yourself to an ongoing effort of increasing your intentionality. The great thing is, some of this eventually becomes second nature. It's not like every single decision is some cumbersome process. Eventually you just know it's a good idea to drink water, and you pretty much know how much water to drink, for example. Eventually you just establish new habits, and a rhythm of behaviors and choices. This raises the bar of the level of where your cups tend to remain just as a default, and from here, you will have a new, higher foundation upon which you can build further. Here is where the benefit of acting sooner than later shows its head. Start now. It simply takes time to establish who you are, who God has called you to be, the foundation of you, that unique person, and the "perfection" (King James word for maturity) of that person. There will be pleasures, pains, challenges, victories, and defeats along the way. But begin the intentionality now, so that you can begin receiving the feedback needed to make the necessary adjustments to your choice machine/ decision making process, with enough time that the adjustments are truly meaningful and helpful. The better you become at this feedback loop, and at choosing the right combination of sacrifices/ investments, the more authority and power you will eventually command with your words and actions, the greater the impact you will have in the lives of others, and the greater the impact you will make for the kingdom of Heaven.

Free Will and Language Fill Your Wellness Cups

So far, we have explored the origins of Free Will and Language, we've looked at many of the sub categories, and have begun to understand how to exercise/ use each. It was necessary to lay this foundation in order to truly empower you to get the most from the remainder of this series. In order for you to unlock and absorb the power that is contained in this series, you first have to read it, understand the language, process and retain the language, and then choose with your free will to engage and continue engaging. In order for you to walk away from this book, and have the investment of time and energy produce any degree of benefit in your life, you will be required to make an incredible number of choices, and you will need to command language to serve you. There are a few remaining nuances that will be helpful for you on your wellness journey. Turn up your focus for a few more minutes, and I will try to help you leverage what we have learned regarding free will and language. The few remaining distinctions in this chapter are quite powerful, sadly missing from most people's understanding, and largely missing from their conversations. These remaining distinctions are simple, but profound. Lacking understanding of these distinctions is a strong contributor to the lack-of-power condition from which most people live their lives.

Listening

A dictionary will define listening as: "giving one's attention to a sound", or to "make an effort to hear something". I believe there is much more depth to the concept of listening than just giving your attention to a sound vibration with your ear(s). I have chosen to take "listening" to a much deeper level, and I believe that commitment has made all the difference in the world for me in my pursuit of wellness.

I perceive that the overwhelmingly vast majority of people pay little-to-no attention to their surroundings. Most people are completely focused on themselves, whether it's the thoughts they are having, the signals they are receiving from their flesh (I'm hungry, I'm bored, I'm tired, etc), or the cellphone or TV in front of them. This is evident constantly in conversation. Have you ever been talking with someone, and their response painfully and clearly shows how little they were paying attention? We've all experienced this at some point. There are varying levels of distraction, though they may not all be as blatant. Sometimes people don't respond at all, even when the volume and proximity of your speaking should have been more than adequate for them to hear you. Sometimes they answer your question with an unrelated question, effectively dismissing your question. Sometimes when you are telling a story or making a point, you can kind of see a glazed look over someone's eyes, and the moment you are done talking, they erupt with the thought they were so "politely" waiting to make, but clearly showing they gave zero thought to what you shared. Failing to respond to multiple questions in an email (even when bulleted and truncated) is a common workplace phenomenon. I've often been quite disappointed with the level of listening I've encountered from employees, colleagues, customers, bosses, vendors, and even professionals who are supposed to be the cream of the crop when it comes to "attention-to-detail" like computer engineers, accountants, brokers, and attorneys. Most people somewhat expect and excuse poor communication from young, low-pay hourly employees, but I was surprised to find the same communication failures are present with C-level executives earning $2000/hr. Very few people, who I have encountered, operate from a place of super high integrity when it comes to listening. It's tempting, but short-sighted, to dismiss these unfocused people as unintelligent, or to become offended, choosing to believe that they intend to ignore you from a place of intentional disrespect. Your flesh is somewhat hardwired to become frustrated, and to take offense, when you are in the middle of a situation tainted with poor communication. But we can take a step back, give the person the benefit of the doubt, and try again. I believe we are all capable of improving the level of listening we are choosing, and part of that capability is the capability to listen past our offenses. See, hear, and taste the situation; likely you will find the person has failed to listen well, or respond thoroughly, because they are pulled in many directions and they have allowed their focus to be divided ineffectively. Rather than take offense with the person, choose to empathize, relate to them and their place in the situation, and choose patience. It may be that you will sometimes, or even often, carry the weight of the conversation, email, or text when details are critical and accuracy is necessary. Welcome again to the burden of leadership. Rather than choosing offense, choose forgiveness. You can also choose to be thankful that you have been empowered with greater listening ability than others. Few people listen and communicate well, and even fewer people have the patience to forgive each other, move on, and press forward with a positive attitude. The result is slow progress, poor productivity, missed opportunities, and burned bridges. It's a handicap affecting the majority of our population, and most are completely unaware. Let's take a closer look at a higher functioning, more helpful form of listening, "Listening", and how to unlock the utility contained. I believe we can distinguish Listening both as a graph, and as a spectrum of focus.

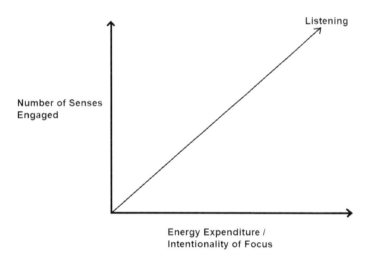

I won't belabor this point too terribly. You are probably able to understand some level of what I'm trying to say with the graph without an extensive written analysis. Basically, your Listening increases as you engage more of your senses and focus. But don't breeze past this point. While simple,

the implementation of this Listening concept is difficult and requires much effort.

This inherent difficulty results in a preponderance of poor Listening. The poor Listening creates poor communication, less knowledge, poor decisions, damaged trust, less intimacy, a lack of power, increased chaos, and unfortunately sometimes even death. The great news is, the engagement of more senses and focus becomes easier through exercise. The more frequently you choose to increase your Listening intensity, the perceived effort does eventually become somewhat less than it was initially, and the practice can become more habitual. Through habitually raising the bar of what you expect from yourself, in regard to the quality of your Listening, you will raise the base level from which you typically tend to operate. You eventually become someone that most people would describe as "a great listener". I've found that my willingness to engage a higher level of intentionality toward Listening has resulted in a very high level of trust and intimacy in all of my relationships, even with people I have just met. We will go into more practical coaching on becoming better at Listening in many of the other chapters, because this concept is critical for pouring into your wellness cups. Your body, the people around you, and your environment are CONSTANTLY giving you invaluable feedback. Most people sadly make little effort to tune in to receive that information. Some of it is free information. Some of it actually costs you much to produce, and you still ignore it. The information you need to make wise, powerful, helpful, and impactful decisions is all around you. There are trees full of low hanging fruit all around you, and most people are starving because they won't even bother themselves to look up. Part of this lack of focus is a lack of training, part of it is laziness, and part of this is an intentional attack, with poor Listening being intentionally woven into our society through culture, technology, and entertainment, keeping most people weak, isolated and enslaved.

The senses I'm referring to on the previous chart are your basic physical senses (sight, hearing, smell, taste, and touch) plus spiritual and emotional sensitivity. We will discuss ways to increase your awareness and sensitivity spiritually and emotionally later, but for now, just consider that when I describe Listening, it's an all-hands-on-deck approach. Optimized Listening receives the maximum number of inputs available, and receives them to their full extent. There is an opening of one's heart, soul, and mind at the higher levels of Listening. This higher level of Listening creates higher meaning, and greater levels of possibility. At the highest levels of Listening, when you have shut down all of your own internal dialogue and silenced all distractions, you open up your spiritual doorways and let down your defenses. This can be good, but you are actually vulnerable in this place, so the highest levels of Listening should only be reserved for those people you trust deeply. The highest levels of Listening allow not just the transfer of ideas and information, but also the transfer of spirit. There is an open highway with no speed limit for traffic. This presents a responsibility for wisdom and discernment to guide the level of Listening you choose in each situation, in each environment, and with each person or group of people. Choosing the correct level of listening where you gain all of the information that is helpful, without picking up/ gaining anything that is unhelpful (false information, lies, evil spirits) in every situation becomes the goal. Most people won't reach the highest levels of Listening. Since much of the process of Listening is a personal journey, I won't even be able to coach you to the upper 90th percentile, much less to complete mastery, but I will do my best over the course of this series to point you in the right direction, and give you a decent push that way. If you take the "Listening" line from the graph and lay it out flat, you could effectively create a space where you could plot yourself (or compare yourself with others) on your current Listening location. Your location on this spectrum is constantly shifting (SQUIRREL!). This tool is somewhat limited in utility. The main helpful thing I think this tool can do for you, is to remind you to actively choose to engage more of your senses, and to remind you to be more intentional. Anything beyond that (comparing yourself to others for example) is likely just unhelpful fleshly pride.

LISTENING
Spectrum of Focus

Poor Focus
with few senses
engaged

⬅️━━━━━━━━━━━━━━━━━━━━━━➡️

Excellent Focus
with all senses
engaged

⬆️   ⬆️

Are you currently here?   or here???

It's also true that there are SIMULTANEOUSLY a nearly infinite number of Listening spectrums going on with you at any given moment. This is because we are surrounded by people, objects, and spirits, and each individual entity has the ability to capture some level of your attention. There exists a Listening Spectrum of Focus between you and each and every one of these entities. Some of them are actively campaigning for your attention. Some of them seem to draw your focus energy toward them. And some are not demanding or asking for any attention whatsoever, but we can still choose to gift them some of our focus (for example, in the middle of a battle in war, a soldier could choose to stop looking for the enemy, and just sit down and stare at a piece of pine straw. This choice is not likely to be helpful if you are truly committed to surviving a firefight and/or subduing your enemy. We're constantly surrounded by "pine straw"). If you were able somehow to accurately measure and graph the level of focus you were giving each person, object, or spirit around you, there would be a massive nest of Listening Spectrum of Focus lines surrounding you. Some of the lines are pulling your attention out of you, like a car that is out of alignment pulls the driver to one side of the road. The challenge becomes:

1) how to correctly prioritize which line presently really needs your attention, and how much of that attention you should invest/spend (based on the goals you are committed to presently, or the activities/ possibilities in which you have enrolled yourself)

2) how to correctly assess the needs of multiple (all that are present) focus lines (each person, object, or spirit)

3) how to avoid/resist inappropriate or unhelpful (inconsistent with goal achievement/satisfaction) distractions

4) how to powerfully command control over the focus of each line to actually produce the desired result

It's madness, really, what is constantly going on, and this difficulty or complexity is the reason most people fail so miserably at Listening. It's almost like there is a production studio mixing board in front of you, and you are constantly responsible for tuning and tweaking the levels of the knobs in front of you as all of your inputs (singers, instruments, lights, smoke machines, etc.) are all out there frequently changing their levels of outputs to you.

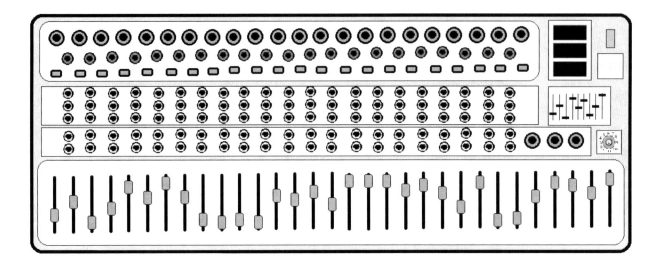

We all get on some level that we are all juggling, and doing our best to prioritize and slice up portions of our attention. Unfortunately, most people spend most of their time frantically working the mixing board, going back and forth, wondering why they are struggling to hear and see clearly what is being produced (sound from speakers and video on the screen), because they neglected to notice and increase the main gain knob that limits the output of the entire board. Through practice and intentionality, you can actually increase the amount of focus you are generating. Then, even though you are still slicing up your focus pie into many slices, the amount of pie on the plate is larger, even though still thinly sliced, because the pie itself is larger! Turn your overall energy focus knob up, and generate more electricity within your brain, so you are able to really pull a greater amount of information from the people, objects, and spirits you select. Or don't, just know either way that the main gain knob has a spring in it that is designed to turn your overall focus energy down to a mundane level, so a person who accepts the challenge/ opportunity to increase their focus must frequently choose to apply the correct pressure to the main gain knob to keep focus levels high. The degree to which you understand and take control over your ability to not just direct your focus, but also to GENERATE focus, will determine the amount of information you are able to receive, and therefore the degree to which your decision making is informed, eventually affecting the quality of the outputs your decision making produces, and eventually contributing toward (or limiting) the extent of the enterprise and legacy (earthly and heavenly fruit) you are able to build (grow and harvest).

For some, a moment to reflect on their Listening skills would be helpful here. Does anyone ever tell you they think you are a good listener? Do people have to repeat themselves often with you? Do you ever find yourself in longer, more intimate discussions? Do people share details with you? Do people feel safe enough with you to be vulnerable? Do you feel confident enough in your Listening skills to be vulnerable with others? Do you have the wisdom to know when to open yourself up and when you should close yourself off? Do you have discernment to understand there are degrees to all of this? What level of command or control do you believe you have over your Listening? How focused have you been in your Listening so far while reading this book? Do you think there is a stronger level of focus you can muster going forward?

Perhaps it's helpful and appropriate at this moment to declare out loud,

"I am capable of improving my Listening skills!"

"I am committed to improving my Listening skills!"

"I will improve my Listening skills!"

"I AM IMPROVING MY LISTENING SKILLS!"

It really is all about what "works". A machine works when all of its components are present and in the right place. The machine either functions perfectly, at some level of inefficiency, or it is off entirely. What we are doing by Listening is trying to pull together all of the necessary pieces of the puzzle/ machine and trying to put them in their correct place, so the machine works the best it can. Without Listening, often we fire up a machine that is missing parts, and then we wonder why there is a break down. The same is true regarding the filling of all of our different cups, and should inform our goal setting and moment-by-moment choices. Does this choice "work" with the machine I'm building? If I wanted to build a different machine, which parts (or choices) would I need, to put this thing together? We will continue to distinguish each wellness cup, and what truly "works" with each machine/ cup as we march our way through this experience/ book together.

The act or process of Listening gives you greater access to helpful information, and makes your decision-making/cup-pouring efforts more helpful, more powerful, and more efficient. I've also found that simply engaging in the process of active Listening creates value all by itself. Even before any decisions or actions have been taken, value has been created simply by entering into Listening, especially when it comes to the social component. Since Listening is unfortunately so rare these days, and people love to talk and have people listen to them, just simply being a person who is more focused and receptive will cause many people to be drawn to you. I've found that EVERYONE likes to be listened to. This doesn't mean that everyone wants to engage at a high level. True Listening would pick up on the level of attention someone wants from you, how much eye contact they are comfortable with etc, but at whatever level someone wants to communicate with you, when they do, they want some level of listening to take place on your part. Choosing to be someone who Listens well, as an ongoing standard mode of operation, means that you will be someone that most people instantly, or at least quickly, accept connection with, like, admire, and trust. We will expound on this blessing later.

The entire "Listening" section is so important, you should probably go back right now, before moving on, and read it through again. This time, try sitting more upright, turn off any unnecessary audible noises near you, take several slow deep breaths, make sure the ambient lighting is bright enough to be helpful, but not so bright as to be painful or a distraction, and try reading it more slowly, with as much focused intentionality as you are currently able to create. You may even want to highlight portions that stand out, or take some notes. The best way to begin to process more of this would be to try to teach someone what you believe you learned from this section. Then, have them actually read this section. Then, take the time to discuss with them what they got out of your teaching and their reading of the Listening section, and then reflect on the total experience and share back with them. You would gain more and more depth of understanding the more times you do this. Including additional individuals in this process with you over time also helps you to gain perspective from multiple angles, resulting in a more complete look at the actual, full, real picture of Listening.

Integrity and "I'll Try"

Another important language distinction that will be helpful for you as you are challenged to commit to actions throughout this book is the concept of "Integrity". I've already used the word integrity many times in this book, but we're going to take a closer and deeper look now. As "Listening" is to "listening", "Integrity" is a deeper, more powerful, and more impactful form of the regular word, integrity.

A simple dictionary definition of integrity:
1) the quality of being honest and having strong moral principles; moral uprightness
2) the state of being whole and undivided
   a. the condition of being unified, unimpaired, or sound in construction
   b. internal consistency or lack of corruption in electronic data

These definitions are great and helpful, but we can add to them to create a more powerful and empowering word. "Integrity" does indeed embrace the ideals of honesty and morality. Where we add power is by expanding on "the state of being whole and undivided"; having an impeccable level of "consistency" and "lack of corruption" is where this power is unlocked. I mentioned earlier in the book, that Integrity to me includes the practice of **actually doing** what I say I'm going to do, **when** I say I'm going to do it. At my wedding, my best man told everyone at the reception something to the effect of, ~ "when Jonathan says something, you can take it to the bank." Of course, there are times when I fail to live up to this, but I was thankful to hear someone who knows me so well use those words to describe me. That showed that the intention I have toward honoring my word is observed by others in the way that I interact with them. It shows a positive correlation between the words that I use, and the actions I take. Far too many people take a flippant position when it comes to the words that they use, and the expectations for action that are created. Take a moment to consider the following statements:

- "I will call you back in 5 minutes"
- "I will be there at 7am"
- "Sure, I'll be happy to take the trash out"
- "I will have it built by the end of this week"
- "I'm going to read my Bible today"
- "I'm going to read my Bible for 20 minutes every day"
- "I promise to be faithful to you, until death do us part"
- "If you cross this line, we will impose economic sanctions upon you"
- "Clean up your room right now or else you are in trouble!"

There is a broad range of comments above. Some are words that are spoken between two friends, some between spouses, some between leaders of countries, and some between parents and children. There are literally an infinite number of statements/ commitments we could continue listing, but you should be understanding where I'm at by now. While the severity of the impact of the fulfillment of the spoken commitment varies on many levels, there is always a binary reality created; either the words and actions lined up perfectly, or they didn't. Either the person was out-of-Integrity with their words by their actions, or they were in-Integrity with their words, and the people they spoke them to, by their actions. Either they did, or they didn't. Either they fulfilled/ followed through with/ completed their word exactly, or they didn't. This is

HUGE.

Yes, I'm being obnoxious with my fonts again to get your attention. People shoot themselves in the foot constantly by making verbal commitments that they don't keep. They dishonor themselves, and the people they make the commitments to, when they fail to live up to their end of the words they speak. On some level, they are communicating a lack of respect, a lack of willpower/ ability/ strength, or all of the above when they don't do what they said they would do. This plays out in a number of ways. Failing to call someone back when you said you would, shows them whatever you had going on in your life was more important than they. That's often accepted and excused, but a reality is created, whether it is ever consciously acknowledged or not, especially if this becomes a frequent occurrence. The reality is, the person knows that they are much lower on your list of priorities. Perhaps if this is someone you are trying to shake off, or create distance from, then that is what you are going for. But I've observed this over and over between people that I know actually do care for each other. No matter how small, some level of distrust is planted each time this happens. A wedge gets driven deeper, if even slightly, separating the two people and reducing trust and intimacy. Often this takes place completely unnecessarily. I've often encountered people that speak specific commitments when one wasn't even expected. "I will call you back in 5 minutes" ... and then you don't talk to them for a month. Obviously, the conversation wasn't critical, or you or the other party would have reached out sooner. If there was no real sense of urgency though, why did you commit to something specific? I know I'm already losing the Integrity-zombies right here. "Man, you're making too big a deal out of this". Am I? Or could it be that your habitual failure to honor your word impacts more of your life and your relationships than you understand? Could your lack of Integrity be hindering your professional development, your finances, the partnerships you are able to create, and your occupational wellness? Is your lack of follow-through cheapening your words and making you less powerful? Are you confused as to why your children won't follow your instructions? If you are feeling defensive here, there is a high likelihood that you already know you are an Integrity-zombie. You know it sucks when you don't do what you say, but you don't want to take ownership for it. Your "dominate and avoid being dominated" flesh suit is controlling the situation, rather than you bringing your flesh into submission humbly, by acknowledging your failure to speak and act powerfully with Integrity. Acknowledging there is a problem is the first step in solving the problem, right? Also, often just the simple act of owning the failure with the person with whom you are out-of-Integrity, removes the wedge of distrust. Most people, especially people who love you, are willing to forgive you if you ask. But it's uncomfortable to expose deficiency. It's embarrassing for most to admit even small failures. I know some people who refuse to say they are sorry, no matter how wrong they are. Even when they know they are wrong, and make some level of effort to clean it up, the effort is an obvious charade, and the language they use not only shirks responsibility, but further insults the person they have already offended. People do this constantly with unnecessary commitments, and suffer detrimental effects in their relationships. How much worse is the damage when more is really at stake in the commitment? Sometimes, terrible suffering occurs for many people when a spoken word is not honored by a corresponding act of completion.

Obviously, most people aren't drawing lines in the sand, or signing contracts where the fate of nations and the lives of millions hang in the balance. But most people operate from a place of speaking, and failing to actually fulfil the words they speak, CONSTANTLY. Some people at least recognize their propensity toward failing to complete what they say, so in an effort to avoid being out-of-Integrity, they will use the cop-out of, "I'll try". People think this better. In a sense it is, because it's not making a liar out of you, so you're at least not cursing yourself from failing to complete your "mini" oath/ covenant. But it still weakens and cheapens your word. It still weakens and cheapens who you are, and the level of Integrity people know they can expect from you. I guess we're back to our "good, better, best" scenario. It's good avoiding committing to something you won't complete, it's better to speak a commitment and actually fulfill it to the T, and it's best to do this all the time, every time you speak. Obviously, this is an ambitious and lofty goal, but the degree to which you nail this will determine the power in your words, the trust in your relationships, and ultimately the level of opportunities or assignments you will have the privilege of saying "yes", or "no" to. I had to maintain a high level of completing my commitments and honoring my word over the course of many, many years to even begin to qualify as a person who would be approved for loans and a commercial real estate lease for my first business. It took me over a year and many loan applications before I was able to secure financing and a lease for my gym. I barely squeaked in, but after several years of solid performance and demonstrating that I would fulfill and complete any "Yes" I made, I had lenders, franchisors, and landlords contacting and soliciting me with much more favorable terms. New opportunities were created as a result of my faithfulness. I demonstrated a high level of Integrity, and the truly successful people in life understand with greater clarity that Integrity really is everything. If you can find someone who will actually do what they say they will do, no matter what, that person is nearly unstoppable, an invaluable asset to your team, and a much less risky investment. The same is true regarding every person with whom you interact. People are drawn to people who honor their word. Opportunity is created. Growth happens. Life thrives and perpetuates. Things "work". We all understand on some level that the inverse is true, and sadly much more common. When people don't honor their word "it" whatever "it" is at hand, doesn't work. This damages trust and destroys opportunity. Chaos grows and life suffers. Nobody really wants to be part of that, though most people actively contribute heavily toward this less fortunate reality.

This Integrity conversation is not just for improving your interactions with others. It's also a conversation about holding yourself more accountable. Part of the reason I've harped on this so long here, while we are still setting the framework for the wellness conversation, rather than waiting to introduce Integrity later, is that this concept literally affects all of the wellness components. It is just as important that you honor your word with yourself, as it is to honor your word with others. If you make a commitment to yourself, the same order and chaos fork-in-the-road paths are created. When you honor your word with yourself, both in the small and in the large commitments, life and order are created. When you fail to complete your word, even with yourself, chaos manifests in your life; disorder and death become one step closer. So, before the time spent in review of the technical lists of dos and don'ts for each wellness component can be helpful, it is necessary for us to take the time to address how you find the power to "do", and how you find the power to "don't". It's with our words. Remember all power is God's, He simply gives us the authority to do things here. We have authority when are in-Integrity with God's Word, with others, and with ourselves. Here's a little (HUGE) equation for you:

BEING IN-INTEGRITY WITH GOD'S WORD

BEING IN-INTEGRITY WITH OTHERS

<u>+   BEING IN-INTEGRITY WITH YOURSELF</u>

AUTHORITY

If you take any of the three out of the equation you decrease the amount of authority present from which you can operate. It's a plus sign rather than a multiplication sign, because nobody is perfect and if we drop the ball even slightly, a multiplication sign would negate all authority to zero. God is more gracious and merciful than that. He understands the wicked, lazy, selfish nature of the meat-suit we inherited. He gives us many chances to pick ourselves up and try again. At some point as we mature from children to adults though, the decisions we make to honor or dishonor our word begin to create our realities. It becomes harder and harder to rebound and/or rebuild. At some point, there is a separation among those in the race. Those who consistently honor their word pull ahead. Those who consistently dishonor their word fall behind. How consistently are you speaking and acting in a way that "works" for building the life you want? How consistently are you speaking and acting in a way that "works" for being obedient to your calling? Will you finish your race with excellence and one day hear, "well done, thou good and faithful servant"? Luke 16:10 is worth repeating. All of the following scriptures should terrify and motivate those lacking Integrity. Raise the bar. Raise your level of expectation for your level of Integrity. If you say you are going to do something, DO IT. Even if it is uncomfortable or you underestimated the cost, DO IT. The lies that "it doesn't really matter that much", or "it's not really that big of a deal" costs us so much more than we can understand. If you ever do drop the ball, OWN IT. Acknowledge where you failed, specifically with the person you let down, and ask them genuinely and humbly for forgiveness. And then next time... "do" better.

He that is faithful in that which is least is faithful also in much: and he that is unjust in the least is unjust also in much.

Luke 16:10

But let your communication be, Yea, yea; Nay, nay: for whatsoever is more than these cometh of evil.

Matthew 5:37

Go to now, ye that say, To day or to morrow we will go into such a city, and continue there a year, and buy and sell, and get gain: Whereas ye know not what shall be on the morrow. For what is your life? It is even a vapour, that appeareth for a little time, and then vanisheth away. For that ye ought to say, If the Lord will, we shall live, and do this, or that. But now ye rejoice in your boastings: all such rejoicing is evil. Therefore to him that knoweth to do good, and doeth it not, to him it is sin.

James 4:13-17

Selah

"AND", "MEANING", "POSSIBILITY", and "STORIES"

As we distinguished "Listening" from the more common "listening" and we distinguished "Integrity" from the more common "integrity", we're going to play around with words again here to hopefully give you some powerful language tools, with which to tackle the wellness bear ahead. This time we are not necessarily creating a new word, but rather unpacking in greater detail the meaning already contained in a word, which is usually grossly overlooked. The word is "AND". Often in language we separate ideas with words like, "and", or "or", or "but". The word "AND" is a very special word with unique power. "And" allows what was spoken or written both before and after the word "and" to be true. Right now, I am writing a book, and I am chewing gum, and I am sitting at my desk, and I have a glass of water next to me, and it is a pretty day today. Every section of words in the previous run-on sentence separated by the word "and" is true, regardless of what the other section is saying, and the addition or removal of one of the sections would not change the meaning or negate the validity of the others. If you can understand this, and recognize where this comes up in conversation (with yourself in your head and with others), you will gain a very powerful tool for communicating: speaking more powerfully so you can be a blessing to yourself and others. There will be times that the understanding of this "and" distinction will be the difference in the building up or the burning down of relational bridges. There will be times that the understanding of this "and" distinction will determine whether or not you are successful in accomplishing your goals and pouring into your cups. Begin to be aware of the language that you use, and the meaning you are assigning to people's actions. Many times, we choose to assign the meaning of an "or" or a "but", which are exclusionary and negating in nature, when an "and" could have been chosen as a more accurate and helpful relation to an event. Let's go through a few scenarios to illustrate:

Scenario #1
Husband and wife are both stretched thin with work and home duties. They have argued many times over the wife asking the husband to carry his shoes to his closet, rather than leaving them in the middle of the floor. It happened yet again, and the wife is furious. Obviously, if he really loved her, he would remember to pick up his shoes, and would make the effort to move them where she has asked, right? She begins to create the meaning in her head surrounding the event of: hubby leaving shoes out = that he doesn't love her. She freaks out on him. He apologizes and says he is sorry that he forgot. She doesn't accept his apology because to her, the apology is obviously just a weak attempt to lie and manipulate, and he is obviously doing it on purpose. Now, it is possible that all of this is true, but it is also possible that a different reality is actually true.

It's possible that the husband left his shoes on the floor AND that he genuinely forgot.

It's also possible that the husband habitually leaves his shoes on the floor AND that he really does feel sorry about it, and still loves her very much.

If wifey continues to process everything that husband does through the filter of that he "doesn't care" or whatever negative meaning she is creating, the relationship will continue to suffer and could eventually completely break down. If she chooses to process the event through the lens of the other possibility, that he genuinely cares about pleasing her and letting her down, and is still just failing, then she is likely to have a little more patience in the tank, and is likely to continue working with him until they find a solution to the problem or upset that works for them both. It might be as simple as her greeting him with a smile and a hug when he gets home, and asking him to do it right away. Or it might be the placement of a chair in a strategic location or even a little sticky note until the new habit is formed. The point here is not to explore different solutions, or to even take sides. The point of this illustration is to think about the way that we all choose to relate to people and events around us.

Now let's keep looking at scenario #1 from the other side. Husband works hard all day. He doesn't think it's a big deal that he leaves his shoes out. He thinks his wife should either pick them up when she wants them moved, or she can wait until he remembers to and wants to. He feels bad, but he still really kind of thinks she is over-reacting.

I'm not taking sides here and saying that she is or isn't over-reacting. But consider for a moment, that in this case maybe she is over-reacting (maybe the desired placement is literally one inch away from where he is placing them and she has some hard-core OCD struggle or something).

In this scenario it is also possible that he could choose a more powerful and compassionate relation to the entire situation.

It's possible that his wife is overacting, AND that he could still put in more effort to do what she is asking.

You see what happens here when people allow two things to be true in the framing of their perception of an event, situation, behavior, or character? Compassion and mercy prevail, and people get a chance to try again.

Most often, the cause of upsets or altercations between people are the result of the assignment of meaning. One person can assign meaning to an event, and another person can assign a completely different set of meanings to the exact same event. For example, in some parts of the world, showing someone your palm is the same as giving someone the middle finger in the US. In the US, waving your hand is considered friendly. Actually, sometimes if you don't waive you are culturally considered rude. We see in this example that the action itself is not where the offense is derived, but in the meaning assigned to the action. This happens over and over again in relationships. It is a common occurrence between individuals, and is even more common between different cultural groups. This inherent flaw in communication is exploited as often as possible, by people who want to generate money, or even chaos. When you look at our news and social media feeds, nearly every single story or post can be polarizing. How can this be the case, when we all pretty much want the same things, to be safe and loved, and to have a healthy family? It's because of the power of language. Someone skilled in the use of words can create two opposing realities in the same space. Then, isolate the language which is being used on one side of the argument to one group, and promote a different set of opposing words to another group. Both have complete buy in, and from a certain perspective both are right. But if we all take a moment to step back and look at the situation, we will recognize that we all win when we are willing to adjust our perspective. Obviously, there are times when people will outright lie and reject truth. That's not what I'm talking about here. I'm talking about having the maturity to be willing to pause before assigning meaning, to make sure that you have it right, and that your perspective is not only right, but is also going to create the results that you want. Sometimes everyone including you wins, when you first let go of always being right and assuming the worst about others.

Scenario #2
Mom works hard constantly to serve and satisfy her home. It seems/occurs to her that everyone is unappreciative and takes her for granted.

It is technically possible that this is indeed true. Perhaps her family, husband and children all take her for granted, and have a very little amount of genuine appreciation for what she does.

Now, she could just stay with the internal dialogue that says "They're so unappreciative". Period. She can place a period at the end of that sentence and it is left in the negative. That negative seed could grow until some worse situation manifests.

Or,

She could say, "They didn't appreciate it when I did this specific thing for them, AND I will continue to choose to love and serve them anyway".

Boom. Even though the little boogers are acting entitled currently, Mom chose the higher road, and adjusted her language to leave more love and power present. She chose to be more mature and chose to limit her frustration to the one incident, rather than mentally and emotionally dressing the people she is serving in a permanent negative costume that she will see them in from now on.

Usually, people exaggerate in their emotional responses to the actions of others, and assign meaning that is not really there. (*Somebody acted selfishly one time and you painted them with the description of "selfish", and now everything they do looks selfish to you. If you have any authority over them, you actually just cursed them with that condition in your speaking, and now you share the burden of their unfortunate reality*). We will go through more training in the I Am Emotional and I Am Social chapters on the creation and assignment of meaning, and how we can powerfully choose "better" meanings to serve the people and situations before us. But we had to touch on it now, to introduce the power of "AND" before you really step up to the plate and take a swing at this wellness game. You will have less unnecessary weight to carry on this journey, if you can begin to understand the benefit of choosing AND. You leave space for joy and peace to remain, when you choose to assign positive meanings to the actions of others. Not making everything mean the worst meaning you can think of, leaves a greater range of possibilities present. As you go through life, it is usually beneficial to try to make choices that create newer and more numerous opportunities. Order creates opportunities and new possibilities. Chaos produces fewer options. This same mindset is helpful, not just in giving people the benefit of the doubt around you, but also in overcoming obstacles between you and your goals. Some of these obstacles can be self-imposed, some of them can be thrown in front of you by others, and other obstacles could have just been inherent in the game you're playing. Usually when people hit roadblocks or obstacles, they just shut down and give up. The people who make it the furthest in life, are normally those who persist and keep persisting. Often this road of persistence is characterized by a theme of the person regularly considering a "possibility" outside of what they currently know or think to be true. The only way to break through our cognitive dissonance is to be able to "try on" new possibilities like someone would try on a coat. If you find that you like the "coat", you can keep it on. If you don't, you can take it off and go back to who you were before you tried the coat on. The more radically different a new thought process is from the current "story" you are creating, the harder it usually is for people to consider. Since we are constantly assigning meaning to every word someone says (or doesn't say), and every action someone takes (or doesn't take), the accumulation of those meanings strung together eventually paints a picture. Your "story" is being created in your mind. If you happened to get the assignment of a meaning wrong, then your "story", even though real to you, could potentially be inaccurate. The greater the weight of the inaccuracy, the higher the cost/ detriment.

Scenario #3

A person didn't graduate college. They were told by their merciless parent that they would never get a good job. They chose to accept these words as true, therefore they never even applied to the job they wanted. They accepted the curse that someone spoke over them. The "story" into which they have placed themselves doesn't allow for them to consider the possibility that something could be different. It would be a radical shift in thinking to speak powerfully, "I WILL GET A GOOD JOB!". All of a sudden, the speaking of a blessing has broken the power of the curse, and they begin writing and telling themself a new story. In this new story, the character they play actually CAN get a new job. The person had to first believe that getting a new job was possible. Once they are actually aware of the possibility, then they are in a position to seek after, and obtain, the opportunity that was there all along, previously without being realized.

Our lives really are similar to the movie The Matrix in this regard. In the movie, people are plugged into a machine where the reality they experience is not real, but it is indistinguishable from reality to the person, so they think what they are seeing/ experiencing actually is reality. Some people eventually get unplugged and learn what is happening, and then they learn how to control the machine (to an extent) to serve them. They go back into the Matrix and create realities that are useful to them, and they try to help other people choose to become unplugged. I am doing the same thing here. Most people have a very rigid view of their reality. They "really can't" do xyz. And so, they don't try. As we make our way through this book, you will be presented with many opportunities to consider new ideas, new actions, new habits, and new ways-of-being. If you immediately shut down your thinking due to the story in which you see yourself, then the power available in this book will not occur to you like it is possible for you. You might hear yourself say something like, "well that might work for others, but not for me". And maybe you are right. Maybe something I suggest doesn't work for you. But do you really know if you don't even attempt what I've suggested? As I am providing suggestions from my experiences, I am literally creating new possibilities for you. You have an opportunity, and the power, to feed and water those new possibilities to see if they will grow, or you can stomp on them, pour gasoline on them, and set them on fire with your words. Even if you find yourself saying something in your head like, "oh man I wish that could be true but there's no way I could do that", there is still power in SPEAKING OUT LOUD what you want to be true. So even if you heard a defeated sentence in your head, recognize that and keep the possibility alive by speaking out loud something like, "I believe that is possible, and I'm going to give it my best!". Throughout this series we will go on the offensive, and help you attack and remove the lying, deceiving voices from your life. Some of them are people. We will address them in the I Am Social chapter. Some of them are people without bodies (demons). We will destroy and remove them from your life in the I Am Spiritual chapter.

We will work through more scenarios to clarify and distinguish "and", "meaning", "possibility", and "story", as we make our way through this I Am Well series. For now, I hope you are starting to understand all of these plays-on-words for what they are; we're simply adding a layer or two to the word that already exists. We're describing a slightly deeper truth that is largely lost from all modern cultures: the ability to break outside of your comfort zone (even though most people are actually quite uncomfortable where they are), the ability to humbly consider that maybe you don't have everything perfectly figured out, the confidence in yourself, and faith in God's goodness, to believe that what you are currently experiencing could not only be different, but much better. We've taken so much time here (although we've still only barely scratched the surface) to analyze language, because some of the chains on your life are so powerful that without these language tools at your disposal, the likelihood of your breaking out of them, out of your story and into the promised land, is very small. But WITH these tools in your toolbox, literally everything becomes possible. As soon as you really begin to understand what is possible for your life, and believe that it truly is possible for you, the possibility becomes way closer, and actually within reach. Will you continue on this journey with me to dig deeper into the possibilities that are present for you, your life, and the lives of those you love? I hope so! This poor lost world needs a few more warriors who are willing to take upon themselves the burdens and blessings of the overflowing life.

But when he saw the multitudes, he was moved with compassion on them, because they fainted, and were scattered abroad, as sheep having no shepherd. Then saith he unto his disciples, The harvest truly is plenteous, but the labourers are few; Pray ye therefore the Lord of the harvest, that he will send forth labourers into his harvest.

Matthew 9:36-38

Wrapping up Free Will and Language (*for now...*)

We've discussed the concept of two ditches, each containing error, on either side of the road of truth. As a reminder, this risk is pretty much always present with every topic.

Here are a few to avoid with Free Will and Language:

FREE WILL AND LANGUAGE
ROAD/ TRUTH

UNDERAPPRECIATION DITCH

EXAGGERATION DITCH

- We are complete victims of our circumstances and the cards we were dealt. We are powerless to create or choose any of our reality
- Life is completely empty and meaningless. Everything is subjective and relative
- Low self-esteem, complete lack of confidence, lack of effort, depression
- "I have no accountability or responsibility for my words or actions

- There is power in language, and we have great control over most of our life through the exercise of our free will and the mastery of language
- There is absolute truth. There is also a large amount of meaning that is left up to us to decide/ choose individually what works for our lives
- A healthy understanding of our true strengths and weaknesses, and our real abilities and limitations
- Personal responsibility. Co-laboring and co-authoring our story along with our Heavenly Father

- Since we are created in His image, we have the same level of power with our words; we can be God
- Everything is meaningful. The meaning I have chosen is always right and accurate
- Delusions of grandeur, narcissism, over-confidence in personal abilities, self-worship
- I can perfectly dictate my will over everyone and everything around me and create every aspect of my experience in life if I try or "choose" hard enough

We could keep going with the list of course, but we have to move on. Perhaps it's worth taking a moment here though before we do, to ponder on your own this "Road-to-Truth" as it pertains to Free Will and Language and ask yourself:

- Have I under-appreciated the true power of language?
- Where in my life can I speak more positively and powerfully?
- Am I in the habit of cursing myself or others? Do I need to break any curses?
- Is there a blessing that I could speak over myself, or someone in my life?
- Is there a blessing that I could speak right now?
- Have I under-appreciated the power of my free will, and my role in the creation of my "story"?
- Where can I exercise my free-will more powerfully in life?
- What could I choose differently in my life that would create value for myself or others?
- How/ where can I be a blessing and create value?
- Are there any words I can speak, or actions I can take, now, to pour into my wellness cups?

Most people sadly tend to lean toward the underappreciation side of the road, and fall into the ditch of relating to their free will and language as being less powerful. There are others, however, who may find this book in their hands, who have fallen into the other side of the ditch. There are self-help books, companies, and even cults who believe so strongly in their free will, and their power to speak creation, that they essentially end up in witchcraft and idolatry, whether they realize it or not. If, with honest reflection, you know you are one who leans very heavily on belief in your own supreme power, ask yourself:

- Am I trying to manipulate and control others?
- Am I exhausting myself in constantly trying to over-ride my body's natural response to my environment?
- Have I believed a lie that I am something bigger than I really am?
- Have I gotten into some error regarding the truth of who God is, and what my role is as "creator" in my life?
- Have I gotten into some (any) form of witchcraft or idolatry?
- Have I gotten just a little bit too "big-for-my-britches"?

Before we close out this chapter, we will end with a prayer that will start to correct your steering from toward one of these ditches, back to the center of the road of truth as it pertains to Free Will and Language. We will also continue to describe and distinguish these truths as we journey through this I Am Well series together.

We've not yet gotten to the "cup-specific" chapters where we will dial in to focused recommendations for healthy "cup-pouring", but I hope you realize that I've already been pouring into all of your cups here, serving you some strong soup with meat and vegetables. The focusing, reading, processing, and debating of the ideas presented here, have been time and energy sacrifices you have already made to pour into your cups. Before we can build the foundation for the house, we have to go to the store and get the tools we need right? You'll get better at understanding the tools you now have as you use them. You will gain mastery of the hammer as you swing. Eventually you have to show up on the job site. Each day's progress will look different. Sometimes, you work for days and days at building the house, and the progress seems slow. Sometimes your progress is not really visible to others, or even yourself, but each day that you show up and work, progress is being made. Some days you see tremendous progress, and other people even comment at how good the work is looking. Just know that the slow days are part of the process, and the "noticeable-progress days" couldn't happen without them. As you better understand the building (cup-pouring) processes, you will begin to understand the concept of "hierarchy of impact" (to be detailed later in the series), and how each choice you make contributes, or takes away from, each impact. You will become better at prioritizing your time, and more efficient with your energy expenditures. You will speak more powerfully and precisely. You will speak more blessings, and fewer curses. You will responsibly steward your time and talent, wisely and obediently.

Ways-of-Being

We started from the 30,000 ft-high aerial view of wellness, we discussed the basic concept of filling your cups through free will and language, and we've zoomed in pretty close to take a look at the power of individual words. If we pan out just a bit, and look at a group of words, or seasons of your speaking and acting, I believe you will be able to categorize or characterize seasons of your speaking and acting into themes. Sometimes these themes vary from one season to another, but sometimes people are very consistent in the theme from which they operate (different theme when you are younger vs adult, different themes before and after major life changes or events ie when you became saved etc). I shared the saying earlier, "how you do anything is how you do everything", and since your actions and words tend to align with each other, we can consider these themes in life as "ways-of-being". I challenge you to take a look at the list of some different ways-of-being. Ponder them. Challenge yourself to go deep in your exploration of what it would mean if your life, or a season of your life, was categorized by one of these as a theme. What would your life look like, if several of these themes were present? How would different combinations of these themes look in your life, if they were chosen/ manifested together? Here are some ways-of-being from which people can operate their lives (definitely not an exhaustive list, and in no certain order):

- Agreeable
- Disagreeable
- Inspired
- Uninspired
- Lazy
- Go Getter
- Satisfied
- Dissatisfied
- Mocker
- Slanderer
- Murderer
- Thief
- Manipulator
- Pushover
- Fearful
- Gullible
- Risk Averse
- Risk Tolerant
- Risky
- Safe
- Dexterous
- Not Dexterous
- Thankful

- Warrior
- Coward
- Protector
- Destroyer
- Passive
- Assertive
- Aggressive
- Confident
- Courageous
- Timid
- Joker
- Up for it
- Not up for it
- Considerate
- Inconsiderate
- Defiant
- Obedient
- Open
- Closed
- Happy
- Sad
- Angry
- Resentful

- Selfish
- Selfless
- Self-loving
- Self-loathing
- Careful
- Careless
- Present
- Absent
- Punctual
- Tardy
- Eager
- Willing
- Unwilling
- Wise
- Stupid
- Over-achiever
- Under-achiever
- Planner
- Spontaneous
- Strong
- Weak
- Contributor
- Trusting

- Dangerous
- Adventurous
- Forgiving
- Bitter
- Curious
- Obedient
- Disobedient
- Athletic
- Artsy
- Calculated
- Analytical
- Submissive
- Dominating
- Leader
- Follower
- Doesn't take anything seriously
- Takes everything very seriously
- Completer
- Procrastinator
- Yes
- No

I could keep trying to beat this dead horse from multiple angles, but hopefully you see by now that this list is only a partial list and the full list of "ways-of-being" is very long. Some of the descriptors are easy to process in your brain as a theme from which you could live your life. Even some of the more specific or simple seeming words in the ways-of-being chart could actually be a theme from which you tend to act and speak. Some you need to look at more abstractly to see, but they are still there. It's valuable to understand the mode(s) from which you tend to operate, so you can understand if that mode is actually helpful to you. Is the way you tend to see the world, and interact with it, helpful for achieving the life you want? Is the way you tend to operate, consistent with accomplishing the goals you set? Is the way you tend to "be" a hindrance to the assignments God has given you? Is there a different "way-of-being" which would be more helpful in the completion of your assignments, or for the life you want to create? Most of us default to one of these ways-of-being as a defense mechanism when we are young, in response to our realization of the dominate/ avoid domination arena into which we have been placed. Then, we operate our lives wearing this same jumpsuit everywhere we go. Sometimes the jumpsuit is helpful, and other times it's a hindrance to our activity or our mission. It is the truly emotionally intelligent person who is able to "change clothes" so that your "apparel" is suited best for the environment. Is the environment around you cold and harsh? Is it warm and welcoming? If you prepare for the harshest of environments because you grew up in Alaska, that might suit you well if you still live in Alaska, but if you have now moved to Florida, you're going to need to take off the parka, and put on a swim suit if you want to absorb some of the sun and be able to swim efficiently. Similarly, people grow up in abusive homes or neighborhoods and develop a hardened exterior, but then when they have moved away from the abuse, they aren't able to "wear" a different way-of-being so they can let the kind-hearted person in front of them near them. They may suffer from loneliness as a result of the hard-exterior they have put on. Sure, this hard-exterior protects them from danger, but also keeps them from feeling the warmth of the sun or the cool refreshing of the water that is unique to the new location where they relocated. This is just one example, but you can run with the same illustration with any of the ways-of-being. You were smaller than the other little boys and girls and they made fun of you, so you developed a "sense of humor". This joking way-of-being kept the bullies from picking on you, and made people like you. Now as an adult you can't stop joking, and people don't take you seriously. Even though you are very competent at your job, you aren't getting promoted because for "some reason", those making the promotion decision just don't think you are ready for the seriousness that a leadership position demands. Or fill in the blank. Nobody is able to be a perfect chameleon in every situation and with every person, and I'm not suggesting that you should be inauthentic. But I am suggesting that there are times when your default, especially if rooted in childhood trauma, is not helpful, and that there are other ways you can choose to be that would add value to your life. It's going to be quite difficult to pour into your social cup, if when you suffered abuse as a child you chose to put on a closed-off way-of-being. No matter how many kind, loving, caring, compassionate, safe people the Lord brings near you, you won't be able to love them back, bond with them, and have a healthy relationship grow without changing that unhelpful way-of-being. Consider that you can still decide to put on your closed-off "jacket" again later if you decide to, but that it may be worth the risk to try on a "shirt" which leaves you a little more vulnerable. The same idea actually works across all of the wellness cups, not just emotional and social. As we work through the different chapters, I will try to suggest ways-of-being which are helpful for maximizing the pouring into of that specific cup. You will then have a choice to make; will I choose to try on this new way-of-being and see if it serves me, or adds any value to my life? You have an opportunity, whether you are young or old, to exercise your free will to speak intentionally, act intentionally, and to try on new ways-of-being. At the end of your life, what will people speak about you? Will your life have been characterized by a theme of courage? Of persistence? Of leadership and service to others? Of victory? If these are goals of yours, then you will need to, more consistently than not, choose these ways-of-being as you are confronted with obstacles and opportunities. What sort of changes do you need to make to who you are (or more accurately, who you present yourself as, and operate from) in order to create the legacy you desire? What sort of painting are you painting? What sort of sculpture are you sculpting? If you are not currently acting and behaving as the person that you know you were called to be, it's time to begin the process of creating that person. You may need to shed an unnecessary parka, or put one on, depending on where God has placed you. We will continue to explore this in much greater detail as we go forward, but in order for that process to be of any value for you, you have to get this. **You have the ability to choose.** Not just what you eat for lunch, but also how you *relate* to the idea of eating lunch. You can control the fear you experience to a large degree. You can control the anxiety you experience to a large degree. We can actually destroy the strongholds the enemy has in your life that are causing you to lose power, joy, and effectiveness. To do so, you will need to fight by choosing to

104

embrace a warrior-way-of-being. The greater the courage you choose from which to operate, the greater the breakthroughs, and the greater the victories you will experience.

"Will" you?

Really break that down for a second, is it your "will" to? Will you choose and continue to choose to "be" the way-of-being which actually works for your life? How committed are you? When an enemy comes your way and tries to talk you out of that way-of-being, are you committed to resisting that person and staying the course of continuing to be the person you need to be? "Will" you choose and continue to choose a warrior-way-of-being, until you find victory? I will keep doing my best to give you more tools, but at some point, you will need to choose to use them, or by default you are choosing to not use them. Once you choose, will you continue, moment by moment, to continue choosing the same helpful choice, such that you create a long-lasting, helpful way-of-being?

What is your choice? Right now, in this moment, what is your choice?

What are you showing us is your will?

You won't get it perfectly right all the time. I don't. Nobody can. Only Jesus did. When you act in an unhelpful way, or speak words that are not a blessing, don't beat yourself up, but "do" better next time. God is very gracious and generous with the number of opportunities He gives us to choose. "Do" better. "Act" in ways that are more helpful. Choose ways-of-being that are conducive to success in becoming who you were called to be. Speak blessings. Don't speak curses. Stay on the road, and out of the ditches.

You can do this, with God's grace and through His strength, you really can do this.

YOU CAN BE WELL.

You just have a few choices to make, words to speak, and actions to take to get there.

Will you?

I would like to share just a few more verses to help us wrap up free will and language.

And the tongue is a fire, a world of iniquity: so is the tongue among our members, that it defileth the whole body, and setteth on fire the course of nature; and it is set on fire of hell. For every kind of beasts, and of birds, and of serpents, and of things in the sea, is tamed, and hath been tamed of mankind: But the tongue can no man tame; it is an unruly evil, full of deadly poison.

James 3:6-8

(The verb tense of "tame" is aorist tense, meaning that we will never be able to complete the act of taming the tongue. Does this mean we don't even need to try? NO! This means we have to keep trying; we can never stop trying to tame the tongue if we want to avoid speaking evil)

There is that speaketh like the piercings of a sword: but the tongue of the wise is health.

Proverbs 12:18

Now therefore fear the LORD, and serve him in sincerity and in truth: and put away the gods which your fathers served on the other side of the flood, and in Egypt; and serve ye the LORD. And if it seem evil unto you to serve the LORD, choose you this day whom ye will serve; whether the gods which your fathers served that were on the other side of the flood, or the gods of the Amorites, in whose land ye dwell: but as for me and my house, we will serve the LORD.

Joshua 24:14-15

Selah

Suggested Closing Prayer for Non-Christians: Free Will and Language

(Recommended to be spoken out loud)

God, if you are real, please show me. If all of the stories I have heard about you are true, please confirm for me in a powerful, personal, and supernatural way, so that I have no doubt or confusion in my life regarding who you are. If Jesus really is your one and only son, and somehow, he was actually also you putting on flesh, give me peace to trust that. If you love me, please show me. Please give me a sense of your presence. Please reveal yourself to me. Please give me true faith. If there is only one true path to heaven, please show me and help me find it. Please send your Holy Spirit to convict me of my sins in my heart. Please help me to repent, and find your peace and forgiveness. Please help me to read your Bible. Please show me truth. Please help me to fight the demons that torment me. Please help me to use my free will and language wisely.

Please help me to be well!

In Jesus' name, Amen.

Suggested Closing Prayer for Christians: Free Will and Language

(Recommended to be spoken out loud)

Heavenly Father, thank you so much for this day! Thank you for your beautiful creation of life. Thank you for your kindness. Thank you for your goodness. Thank you for your sacrifice on the cross. Thank you for your resurrection. Thank you for your blood atonement, and for the forgiveness of my sins. Thank you for calling me to repentance. Father, I ask that you would continue to call to me. Please give me your strength to say "yes" to your will. Father let your will be done. Please speak to me, and help me to be obedient to you. Please give me a burning desire to know you more, and to serve you better. Please call me to deeper places, and help me to find you there. Please help me to understand this flesh you have given me, to learn how to crucify it, control it, and surrender my will to yours. Please help me to understand the beautiful gift of free will that you gave to me, and how to responsibly use it. Please help me to understand language better. Please help me to speak blessings over myself and others. Please help me to only curse someone when you have specifically instructed me to do so. Please help me to be a contribution to your kingdom. Please give me victory over all of the unclean spirits, and any evil that will come against me as I read this book. Please protect my family as I study here. Father, I pray that you help Jonathan as he writes this book*. Father, please protect and provide for Jonathan and his family as he tries to do your will here. Help him to avoid teaching error. Help him to use the correct words. Help him to be concise and thorough. Please speak through him. Please help him to be courageous, and to pick up and carry his own cross in this effort. May your will be done in his life also. Keep him close to you, and encourage him through the warfare he is encountering. Father, I pray that you help me to remember everything that is from you. If there are any words here that are not true, or not holy, I rebuke them in Jesus' name! Father, please remove from my brain any words that I have read if they are not true, and please help me to remember all of the true words. Father, again I thank you for my blessed life, and I thank you for the privilege of pursuing you. Thank you for sharing with me. Help me to glorify your name today, and every day. Father, please baptize me with your Holy Ghost, and fill me with your Holy Spirit. Please give me your supernatural gifts of wisdom and discernment to know what is true in my life, and in this book. Please help me to use my free will and language wisely. Please help me to be well!

I love you!

I trust you!

I worship you!

I surrender to you!

All honor, power, and glory are yours both now, and forever!

In Jesus' name, Amen.

Yes, our Heavenly Father is outside of time, so He can answer this as you pray, even after I have written this book!

Chapter 3: The Enemy

Suggested Opening Prayer for Non-Christians: The Enemy

(Recommended to be spoken out loud)

God, again, if you are real, please show me. Please reveal yourself to me in a tangible and supernatural way. Please reveal to me any truth in this book. If there really are any evil spirits attacking me as I'm trying to read this, please protect me from them. If there is anything that is keeping me from seeing you or hearing you, please remove it from my life. If I really do have an enemy, please protect me from him, and help me to gain victory over him. Please be patient with me, protect me, and help me.

In Jesus' name, Amen.

Suggested Opening Prayer for Christians: The Enemy

(Recommended to be spoken out loud)

Heavenly Father, thank you for this day. Thank you for the luxury of this time to read, study, and seek you. Thank you for your sacrifice, and for your blessings of protection and provision. Thank you for your Holy Spirit. Please minister to me, and encourage me. Please expose any deceptions that are active in my life, and any lies I have believed. Please help Jonathan to expose our terrible enemy in this chapter, and help us to gain victory. Help us to trust and have faith KNOWING that Jesus is more powerful than any foe. Right now, in Jesus' name I BIND all unclean spirits in Jesus' name. I bind all lying spirits, deceiving spirits, spirits of confusion and slumber, and spirits of discouragement in Jesus' name. Satan, I REBUKE you in Jesus' name and command you to leave me. You have no power and no authority here in Jesus' name! HalleluYah!

Father, if there are any open doorways, or broken areas in the hedge of protection you have placed around my life, I pray that you reveal them to me, and help me to repent. I pray that you continue to purify me, and refine me in your Holy Ghost fire. Help me to war against the kingdom of darkness. Please anoint me to do your will, and to claim territory daily for your kingdom.

In Jesus' name, Amen.

The Enemy

We haven't even gotten into the tangible lists of things to do and not do yet to pour into your wellness cups, but you are already getting a sense from the previous chapters that the implementation of a wellness lifestyle requires effort, and can be somewhat complicated. Well, unfortunately, the battle is even more difficult than I have already alluded. Every great story has an antagonist, right? As if the process of pouring, balancing, and maintaining your wellness cups wasn't difficult enough, there is a person who is committed to making it even more difficult for you, and he has a posse of thugs that will do whatever he tells them. This person tips the pitcher while you are trying to pour. This person bumps the table and tries to make you miss the cup. He tries to distract you to keep you from pouring, and he will even offer you pitchers of acid, lie to you, and tell you that they are just as good as water for pouring into your cups. *(If you are lost here, you probably skipped ahead and you need to go back and read the chapter, "What is Wellness?" and understand the cup-pouring analogy we will use throughout the I Am Well series).*

For illustration purposes, let's imagine you are trying to create a beautiful painting. This person is hanging around you, telling you that what you are painting is ugly, and that no one will like it. He will say every hateful and hurtful thing he can, to get you to stop painting. If you persist anyway, and remain committed to completing the painting, he will try to get you to change what you are painting into something else. If he can, he will get you to spend your time painting something which ends up being truly distasteful, or disgusting. If he can get enough of your attention, he will talk you into using your talent to paint beautiful pictures of him.

Consider another creative effort; maybe you are trying to build a table out of raw lumber. This person is always distracting you from the job at hand by bumping into you, pushing you, setting dangerous traps for you, yelling in your ear, breaking and hiding your tools, stealing your materials, and bribing anyone you are trusting to help you into sabotaging your work.

Maybe you are trying to learn how to ride a bike. This guy would show up and tell you that squeezing the brakes makes you go faster, and that you don't really need a seat. He would hide in the bushes and throw sticks in your wheel when you go past. He will run at you and try to push you over outright. He will even work so hard as to dig holes in the road in front of you. He lets air out of your tires and reprograms your GPS to take you to a different location than you originally set.

He is a homeless murderer who is bitter and hateful, but given a temporary pass to remain outside of jail. He follows you around, attacks you constantly, tries to steal things that you don't carefully protect, attempts to kill you relentlessly, and is constantly setting fire to your home, your car, and your business. He is fully committed to stealing, killing, and destroying you, your family, your community, and the entire world, spitefully. He actually takes pleasure in every single evil act he can do. Oh, and he just happens to be so powerful politically, that he controls entire nations and commands entire armies.

Now realize this person is invisible.

He is a person in the sense that he has a mind, will, spirit, and emotions. He is just missing a physical body to call his own. He is able to remain completely hidden from view. He is able to go inside some people when he wants, and is able to gain access pretty much anywhere he wants in the world. He has been given access to, and control over, almost all of the world's resources. Unfortunately, he hates you and wants to kill you, even though you may have never met him personally. Does this sound like someone you want to mess with?

I won't be successful at coaching you toward a life of true wellness without teaching you about the reason all of this toil and effort is necessary in the first place. I would be doing you a half-service if I didn't try to expose the biggest threat to your success. If I am choosing to care about others, and have compassion for them, I have to warn them about terrible danger. If I lived in Africa and you were visiting and asked about all the best places to go, I should warn you about the lion that's been eating people before I send you off on an adventure. If I were training you for a boxing event, it would be wise to watch footage of your opponent to learn how he fights, and how best to prepare to defend yourself. Studying your opponent helps you to learn their strengths and weaknesses, and improves your odds of victory. The bad news is, our enemy is extremely powerful, and we don't stand a chance against him on our own. The good news is, JESUS is infinitely more powerful than this chump, and you can have 100% certainty that you will overcome this powerful enemy, IF you submit to the lordship of Jesus Christ, choose to stand courageously, and exercise the power and authority that He gives you. We will go into more on the offensive weapons and defensive moves of spiritual warfare in the I Am Spiritual chapter. For now, in our The Enemy chapter, I am going to do my best to give the terrorist as little air-time as possible, while still fully exposing him and his tactics. A mature understanding of your enemy will give you the greatest odds for victory and success at all endeavors going forward. Most people (especially Christians) are constantly getting sucker punched from the shadows, and don't even fight back.

"The greatest trick the devil ever pulled was convincing the world he didn't exist" – (character Verbal Kint in the 1995 movie, The Usual Suspects. *Derivative likely from a similar quote from Charles Baudelaire in 1864*)

There is some truth to the movie quote. The only power deceptions have is that people believe them to be true. When a person is empowered with truth, they recognize a lie and reject it. When they are ignorant to the truth, they are vulnerable and susceptible to being deceived. When you know you have an enemy, and you know what he looks like and where he is, you can avoid him, or at least get your hands up and prepare to bob and weave when he comes near you. But the sniper hidden in the grass at the top of a hill a mile away is not showing up on your radar. He is able to attack from a distance and limit his risk, and is able to attack on his terms when you least expect it. Your enemy has pulled off some pretty incredible "tricks" or deceptions throughout his existence, and we will expose many of them in this I Am Well series. But it could just be, that the secret sauce for making all of the other tricks work, is that most people still have no awareness of who he is. At best, most people have a very confused and minimal understanding of who he is, and how active he is in the world. It's definitely true that his hobby of tempting and destroying God's children is made much easier by the fact that he is an invisible spirit. This reality is why many people have already lost the battle. They reject the idea that there is both a physical reality and a spiritual reality, that there are both physical beings and spiritual beings. If you are limited in your understanding of reality to only that which is physical, you will continue to remain ignorant of the devices of your enemy, because you won't even be able to acknowledge that he exists. Some people have a belief that some sort of spiritual world exists, but they lack the understanding that there are distinct individual entities within that spiritual world. The concept of good and evil spirits is not just some abstract idea that helps to organize helpful thoughts and behaviors into the "good" category, and unhelpful thoughts and behaviors into the "evil" category. There are literally individual "people" or entities that exist in this realm, who are able to see us, speak to us, follow us around, and yes, sometimes even get inside of us. A very honorable, anointed teacher and preacher, Derek Prince, called demons "persons without bodies". That description was most helpful for me in understanding just what we are up against. And it makes it more personal too, understanding that most of the hardships we face in life are actually just the cause of a person (who happens to not have a physical body) doing something intentionally against us. When I was a freshman in high school, I was invited to go with the varsity football team to a summer strength training camp at the University of Tennessee. One of their head strength coaches at the time gave us some training on the bench press. He said that when he lays down on the bench and puts his hands on the bar, he imagines that the bar is actually a person who is trying to kill him. He said when he does this it helps him to tap into greater intensity. He then proceeded to scream and spit and foam at the mouth as he aggressively pressed some very heavy weight in demonstration (interesting that the word "demon"-stration just came up). The group of young men were all quite excited, including myself, and everyone took turns going as wild as they could on the bar. I embraced his recommendation for several years in training, until I discovered there was greater power, and greater ability to tap into and control my intensity to be found elsewhere (Jesus). While I'm not encouraging this practice of visualization (because it's actually a common practice among the occult, and inferior to the power, might, and strength-to-overcome and create that comes from the Holy Ghost), this memory is still a good illustration. It shows that when someone knows, or at least believes, that a real person is attacking them, they dig deeper and fight with much more ferocity than if they just processed the difficulty in front of them as some removed impersonal event. I hope between this chapter on The Enemy, and the I Am Spiritual chapter, you will understand with much greater clarity that you are in a hostile land surrounded by real, invisible enemies. You don't need to be scared of this fact if you are a real Christian, because, you are the rottweiler and they are the chihuahuas, but I point this out because the rottweiler still must choose to defend itself, or the pack of chihuahua's can still consume him if he is passive and doesn't resist. If you're not a Christian and you are reading this, then I hope you will take away from these chapters an understanding of the source of most of your suffering. God is not to blame for your life's problems. Your real enemy and his clique are. And I'm going to 'splain to you how to "beat-these-fools-down" a little later.

I'm feeling like it's probably a good idea to stop where I'm going for a second.

I have a sense that much of what I plan to write about our enemy will not be received by some of the readers presently. I understand that most people, even many of those who call themselves Christians, are lacking faith. Most people lack the faith to believe that the most High is who He says He is, and they also lack faith to believe that the devil is a real dude with a personality, an agenda, and real power too. I think it's time to share a little piece of my own personal testimony so you can understand how and why I am so fully persuaded that our enemy is real. I'll share more of my testimony later in the I Am Spiritual chapter, but hopefully this next little piece will help you to get more out of this chapter. Hopefully this will help you to engage your enemy more directly, and to fight him more intentionally, with greater intensity. Hopefully my sharing will produce in you an elevated level of faith which will help you to get more out of the remainder of the entire series.

I need to tell you about *chocolate cake*.

Chocolate Cake

I am blessed to have grown up in church. My family (while also quite damaged and imperfect) has a strong heritage of believing in Jesus. My grandmother and aunt on my dad's side were missionaries. My grandpa on my mom's side was a music minister, and my grandma was the church pianist. When I was born, my mom was the church pianist at our church. I spent my childhood growing up in the Southern Baptist church. I went every Sunday morning, Sunday evening, and Wednesday evening, nearly without fail, for the first 16 years of my life. I understood the gospel at an early age, prayed the sinner's prayer, accepted Jesus as my personal savior, and was baptized at the age of 7. I already shared earlier in this book some about my first incredible personal encounter with God at summer camp when I was 14. I also shared some about the unfortunate reality that I ended up straying from my faith as a teenager and leaning heavily into partying. I believed the false Calvinist doctrine of "once saved, always saved, no matter how you live" and gave place to spirits of lust. I said yes to the temptations of fornication and drunkenness and sorcery (drug use). I allowed my insecurities and selfishness to drive me deep down the path of destruction. Through all this self-destruction and sin, I never renounced my faith. If you had asked me if I was a Christian, I would have said "absolutely" and believed it sincerely in my heart. But I was very far from God. I didn't pray much, other than sometimes thanking God for my food. I hardly ever read my Bible. I pushed myself pretty close to death many times. I realized that I was becoming a loser, and the prideful side of me finally realized I needed at least a little balance, and that I needed to get my act together, or I was going to be dead, in prison, or at the very least just extremely poor for the rest of my life. I was prideful enough that this wasn't acceptable. I was selfish enough to want to continue living, and to want some future pleasures enough that I was willing to try to work for it. I was always a very smart kid. I made pretty much straight A's my entire life until my senior year of high school where I failed pretty much every class except English, because that's all I needed to graduate. And even that class I barely passed with a 70 which came down to the final exam. After graduating I continued partying until I was homeless for a season. Finally, this short homeless season was enough of a wakeup call for me to make some better choices. I decided to try to go to college. Even though I destroyed my GPA my senior year, I was still able to squeak through admissions based on my prior achievements and decent SAT scores. I committed to moving fairly far away from home to distance myself from all of the negative influences and temptations that surrounded me. I wanted a fresh start. So, I went off to college and within two weeks I was arrested for drug possession on campus. Now, not only was I in trouble with the law and had even worse financial burdens, I was also on probation with the school and one strike away from being kicked out and homeless again. I knew this was my last chance to straighten myself out. I started making better decisions. I went to class. I started doing my homework. I worked out. I was battling depression pretty hard and spoke with a therapist at the school. To this day I'm still really thankful for this sweet lady. She asked me if there was ever a time that I wasn't depressed. I told her, "Well I guess when I'm busy working". She said, "Well then you could try finding things to keep yourself busy... or I can prescribe you some medication if it's more than you can bear, but you might find that staying busy for a season could help you to pull yourself out of this." I'm so thankful that she didn't just write me a script for some drugs and move on to her next appointment. I thought to myself, "drugs are what got me into this mess, so I don't want to do more drugs. And I know I'm strong enough to tough this thing out, so I will try keeping myself busy". I needed a job and wanted to work at the school's gym. They weren't hiring, but a guy there told me the best chance I would have of getting hired was if I was a certified personal trainer. So, I focused on that. I got certified. I went to class. I finally tried to study and learned how to learn. I started getting A's on most assignments and tests. I eventually got the job at the gym and worked hard to do my best. I showed up on time, did everything with a good attitude, and asked for more work. I was given an opportunity to volunteer to work at my first 5K fun run/race. This was the first time I had ever volunteered my time, and it changed me. For the first time in years, I felt some happiness and a small glimmer of hope. I saw how the selfless efforts that I and a ton of other students made blessed the community. We worked for weeks to prepare for the event, and on the day of the event I was surrounded by hundreds of people who were joyful, happy, and thankful for the event. I saw how we had blessed them, and experienced the blessing that comes from blessing someone else from an authentic place of selflessness. I gained a small sense of hope that maybe I wouldn't be miserable forever, and that maybe I would be able to do something decent with my life. I poured myself and all of my efforts into work, learning, and service. I stayed busy. I stayed SUPER BUSY. My roommates and their friends began making fun of me. I remember one guy saying, "man you're such a do'er... why are you always doing something?". It was true and it made me feel good. This just further strengthened my resolve to "do" even more. I could feel myself getting healthier. I could feel myself getting smarter (gaining ability to tap into, harness, and focus my intelligence). And I saw some fruit in my life from all of this hard work. I was very strong in the gym. I made great grades, moved into a leadership position at the gym, and began making optimistic plans for my future. I was fully committed to being successful by helping people. The wellness vision (although very incomplete) was alive.

While I was still studying in college, I was introduced to an "educational opportunity" with a company whose mission statement was to help people "live life powerfully, and live a life that you love". At this point I was committed to seeking experiences which were rich in opportunity for growth, so it was a no-brainer. This opportunity was basically a several full-day immersion experience that promised to help me radically transform myself into the person I wanted to be, so that I could create the exact life I wanted to live. The training proved to be very powerful indeed. I came away from the long weekend with sharp clarity on the ways I had been limiting myself, and my life, through language and my behavior. I was empowered with a mindset to overcome any obstacle in front of me. I was truly inspired that I could, and would, create the life that I wanted. Many of the lessons I learned through this training have continued to help me in my life with communication, personal relationships, goal setting, and overcoming obstacles. Some of what I learned there is being poured into this book for your benefit. All of this sounds awesome! ... right??

Well, there was just one unfortunate problem with this entire experience. This training cracked the door just barely enough to allow a deceiving spirit in, that planted a seed of disbelief that eventually had me questioning my faith. Part of this training included a focused control over your emotions. The way they accomplished this was through coaching on meaning, and largely this training is true and very helpful. They basically drill into you that life is empty and meaningless, except for the meaning that you choose. And to a degree this is true. One person for example, chooses to assign great meaning to their favorite sports team's success, while their neighbor couldn't care less. And neither person is wrong. That's part of the beauty of life. We get to choose much of our life's experiences and how we will relate to those experiences. All of this is good and helpful. The problem is they carried this teaching too far, crossed the line into blasphemy, and stood for an idea of a reality where God can exist in your head if you choose for him to, or not, and that it didn't matter which way you went with it as long as that choice left you feeling empowered that you were living your best life. This left them the flexibility of catering to every person from every religion. And from a worldly business standpoint, it's a decision that makes sense. Most businesses don't take a stand for a specific religion; in some cases, they can even be sued if they did. But there was so much wisdom and power shared in the rest of their teachings, that I allowed myself to be placed under a spell of sorts. They influenced and manipulated me with their spoken words. Now for the first time since getting saved, I was starting to question my faith. In this training, they really drill into you the ability to consider all things as possible. But this is what the devil does. He will take a biblical truth like "through Christ all things are possible" and change it to "all things are possible". From a certain angle this looks like the same truth, but in reality, the two are worlds apart. So here I am, finally making healthy choices and beginning to thrive, sensing a world of possibilities opening up for me as a young man, being encouraged that the world is my oyster, and I started to hear voices saying things like, "I wonder if that powerful experience I had at summer camp was just another psychedelic hallucination of some kind? Maybe I was just confused about what I was experiencing". Fast forward maybe a year. I had some time to use the new language and emotional tools I had picked up, and was having more and more success in relationships, goal accomplishment, and leadership. I'm kicking butt and taking names, and as on-track as a young man from my humble upbringing could be. I guess I caught the attention of our Enemy and he thought I was ripe for the picking, spiritually. I was enjoying a beach vacation, and had a long conversation one night with a guy while we were looking at the stars. Religion ended up coming up, and I admitted to the guy for the first time ever out loud to anyone that I was starting to doubt the faith that I grew up with. I told him, "I used to be pretty convinced about God and the Bible and all of that, but now I'm not so sure. I don't want to just believe something just because my parents did you know? I want to really know for myself, so I guess I'm still searching for truth". Boom. Little did I know I was being watched, and an assassin was moving in for the kill. With my mouth and the authority given to me in my words, I had just rejected my savior, the Lord Jesus. Like Peter I basically just said, "I don't know the man". Not long after that I went inside and was playing cards with some people. Toward the end of the card game...

Time literally stood still and Satan entered the room.

No, I didn't see some horned red dude with a pitch fork and a long tail. I didn't even see some well-dressed good-looking devil. I didn't see a physical person at all. But I sensed his presence. We talked earlier about description and distinction. There's no way for me to accurately describe the supernatural gift of spiritual discernment for you in a way that you will truly, fully get it. It's something you have to experience to really distinguish and understand for yourself how it is different from other experiences. We will talk in the I Am Spiritual chapter more about the different gifts of the spirit, but for now just know that the Lord can give you spiritual eyes and spiritual ears to see and hear what is going on in the spiritual world. To a degree, at times, people are forcing the veil open into the spiritual realm when they do certain drugs. Some of these experiences are undeniably powerful and profound, unfortunately opening people up to lying and deceiving spirits. It's only when the Holy Spirit chooses to give you temporary sight into the spirit world that you are protected from false information, seeing truth. Sometimes this gift of spiritual discernment can come with visions where you see or hear things. Sometimes the gift of spiritual discernment just comes with a sense of knowing something with absolute certainty. If you haven't experienced this, there is no way for me to convince you, other than to just say that those experiences are more real to me than regular every-day life. Things that God shows to you in the spirit, when it's really from Him, you don't question. You just know. In a similar way that we believe things when we see and hear them in the physical, we believe things we experience in the spiritual when we see them with our spiritual eyes, hear with our spiritual ears, etc. If you came to visit me, how would I know this was true? I would hear the door knock, walk over to it and open the door, see you with my eyes, feel you with my hands if we shook hands or feel you with my body if we hugged. I might even smell you if there was a scent strong enough for me to pick up. You get the point. But after that experience, if I was talking to someone who didn't see you visit, and told them about your visit, what if they didn't believe me? How would I convince them? I would say I saw you, felt you etc. But at some point, they would either take my word for it, or not. There still wouldn't really be a way for me to prove it actually happened without a video of the encounter (which could be computer generated and completely fake too). The same is true with spiritual encounters; we are left with no evidence other than our memories and our testimony, so those experiences are most valuable for us, but much less valuable for others unless they choose to trust you are being truthful. I hope you will choose to trust I am being truthful in sharing this story. Anyway, back to the story. Time stood still and the devil entered the room. I sensed his presence in the same way that I would know the difference if a dog or a cat came in. If a cat came in and left, and you told me it was a dog, I would say you were wrong because with all of my physical senses I perceived the cat. Same here. I perceived Satan to have entered the room and we had a conversation. I sensed he was extremely powerful and truly had the authority to make any deal he wanted. He told me (like he has told so many people before) that he could give me everything I wanted in life. He basically told me I could have the girl I wanted, a great job, power, money, etc. everything that I wanted could be mine, if I would work for him going forward. Friends, at this point I was still partially wondering if this whole thing was a hallucination, and I was finding the experience somewhat humorous and interesting. I kinda wanted to say "yes", just to see what would happen next. The next thing I know there was a large piece of delicious-looking chocolate cake in front of me. The devil told me all I had to do to seal the deal was take a bite of the cake. I sat there for a moment looking at the cake and considering the whole situation, and then HALLELUYAH in the middle of that moment the goodness, graciousness, and mercy of my good, good Father broke into the room with the smallest of whispers, and He whispered three simple words to me:

"This is real"

Friends, all I can say is that instantly in that moment I saw through all of the lies and deceptions that I had entertained. The deception that had taken the devil years to create and build, was instantly destroyed when I heard the voice of the one true God. Three simple words destroyed all the work of the devil, and instantly I sensed just how close I was to the edge of the cliff. I knew without question that the weight of this decision would affect my soul for all of eternity. I KNEW that I was choosing the course for my life, and my eventual destination of either heaven or hell, based on my next response. In that instant I KNEW that the God I had experienced when I was at summer camp was real. I KNEW He loved me. I KNEW the Bible was real, and that I was wicked and pathetic for falling away. I KNEW the Lord was giving me a chance to run to Him, and that He would welcome me back like the prodigal son that I was. I KNEW that the devil was a liar, a murderer, and a thief. I reached forward, took a hold of the plate, pushed it away from me and said, "no". Instantly as soon as I said "no", Satan was gone, time had resumed, and I was back to playing cards.

I wish I could tell you that I was immediately on fire for Jesus again at this moment, but sadly that's not true. I was still pretty lost and didn't know what to do with the whole experience. I no longer had any doubt that God was real, and that Satan was real, but I still didn't have an active, healthy relationship with Jesus, and I didn't know what to do to build one. After this experience I still spent a couple more years in darkness. I entered into a relationship with a beautiful girl who was unfortunately not a Christian. I continued to stay in the sin of fornication and still occasionally got drunk and took drugs. I was still operating from the demonic doctrine of "once saved always saved" and making no personal effort to repent or seek rebuilding my relationship with Jesus. I'll share the rest of this testimony later in the I Am Spiritual chapter, and I will share how I went from being lukewarm, to being **on fire** for Jesus again. I originally planned on just having my full testimony in that one location, but as I was writing here, I felt convicted to share this part of my testimony now. If you took the time to read what I just shared, thank you. Thank you for sacrificing some of your time to hear about a little boy that loved Jesus, allowed the world to distract and confuse him, but eventually found his way home. It's ironic really, that Satan revealing himself to me is what caused me to reject him, and to eventually run home. I guess he isn't as smart as we give him credit for. He really thought I would say "yes", or he wouldn't have exposed himself like that. Really when I "met" him, I thought to myself, "well if Satan is real, then God has to be real too". I'm thankful that even though I don't deserve it, God has revealed Himself to me in many mighty and glorious ways over the years. I will share some more of those beautiful experiences with you as we work our way through the rest of this I Am Well series. I hope that on some level, you can process and receive what I shared about Satan exposing himself, and offering me a deal, as being true and a real event. It's more real to me than most of the rest of my life. I hope that Satan becoming slightly more real to you helps to strengthen your faith, and encourages you to take this whole series, and your whole life more seriously.

Part of me sharing that last experience with you was with the intention of increasing your faith, and part of me sharing that last experience with you was to begin to bring our hidden enemy out from the shadows and into the light. Hopefully it began to shed some light on the reality of his existence, where he came from, who he is, and how he operates; I'd like to go into a slightly deeper analysis on these topics next.

For by him were all things created, that are in heaven, and that are in earth, visible and invisible, whether they be thrones, or dominions, or principalities, or powers: all things were created by him, and for him: And he is before all things, and by him all things consist.

Colossians 1:16-17

If you go back and look at the previous verses starting with verse 12 for context, you will see that the "him' mentioned in verse 16 is Jesus. Jesus was always one with the Father, and from everlasting, meaning that He was not created (obviously he was born as a baby in a manger at a specific point in time, but He still existed outside of that physical body before that). We find out here in Colossians 1 that all things were made for Him and by Him. He is the creator of ALL created things, which includes everything other than The Father, the Son, and the Holy Spirit. This includes Satan. As much as he hates it, he is just a pathetic little inferior created being just like all the rest of the angels, and all of the rest of creation including us, the mosquitoes, and the roaches. God's power is infinite. This means it doesn't matter if an adversary is an ant or an elephant, He is still infinitely more powerful, and technically cannot be defeated. This is really hard for Satan to accept. The story goes that Satan was more powerful and more beautiful than all the other angels. This led to pride and led to him lusting after more power and wanting to be like/as/equal to God. He didn't seek to be more powerful than God, because he was smart enough to know this was impossible. But he wanted to close the gap between his miniscule inferiority and the vast, infinite power of God Almighty.

I will ascend above the heights of the clouds; I will be like the most High.

Isaiah 14:14

The Hebrew word for "like" here is "dama", meaning "to resemble". He just wants to resemble God. That's one reason he hates us so much. WE are made in God's image. Although we are imperfect and much weaker, we still resemble God. Every time he sees a person he is reminded of God, and where he is in the authority hierarchy. Most people have some understanding that Satan is a fallen angel. But did you know that there are different classes/ types of angels? I'm not going to spend a ton of time going into a deep study on angels here, partially because this series is already going to be pretty long with our focus on wellness, and partially because most of the research on angels just produces people's opinions and secular sources. The Bible does indeed mention and even describe angels in many places, but there isn't a ton of detail for us to study that is pertinent to most of our wellness conversation, so I'll limit the time we commit to angels for now. Angels will come up briefly in a few places in the other chapters, but for now I will just mention that in scripture we see angels called: seraphim, cherubim, stars, princes, and sons of God. There is also another distinction called the archangel. Archangel means "chief of the angels". In scripture we only see one archangel specifically, and his name is Michael. There are many who believe there are other archangels. Some people believe that there were three archangels: Michael, Gabriel, and Helel *(Helel is the Hebrew word in Isaiah 14:12 which was translated to Lucifer)*. So, it's possible that Satan was an archangel, and that he used his authority to deceive the 1/3rd of the angels that fell with him. Totally possible, but this is still a speculation. The extra-biblical text of Enoch also apparently describes there being 7 archangels. If archangel means "chief" it's also totally possible that means Michael is the *(meaning singularly)* highest, most powerful angel. Some people use Daniel 10:13 to say there are multiple archangels. In Daniel 10 we see an angel appear to Daniel and told him that he was fighting with the Prince of Persia for 21 days before Michael came to help him. In verse 13 he says, "Michael, one of the chief princes". So, at face value this could mean he is just one of several, but if you study all of those original Hebrew words, it's still possible that Michael is still THE first. The word "one" means "first". And the word "chief" is used in other places of scripture to describe even just random people that were leaders. We only see the word "Archangel" in the New Testament translated from Greek, so it's a challenge to compare the two, since 'chief prince' was written in the Old Testament and translated from Hebrew. It's possible that both are true. Perhaps there are multiple "chief princes", but still only one "archangel". Archangel could just be a title such as CEO, (chief executive officer) in a company. While the CEO technically has the greater authority, there are still other executives in large organizations who have areas they oversee (CFO-chief financial officer, COO- chief operating officer, CIO- chief information officer, etc.) No matter how the responsibilities and authorities are delegated in heaven, God is still the founder and 100% owner of all the shares. Either way, it would be like Helel/ Satan to be jealous of Michael too, and to create a narrative that Satan is more powerful than all the other angels. Maybe Helel was, or maybe he wasn't really the very top angel in terms of power. But he was definitely considered very beautiful and very cunning. Lucifer means light bearer, shining one, and morning star. We know from scripture that the class of angels called morning stars sing songs of glory to the Lord. And the root word for Helel, which was eventually translated to Lucifer, is Halal which means to shine, to flash forth light, to praise, to boast, to make a show, to celebrate and shout. It's also the root for where we get the word hallelujah ('HALAL' 'U' 'YAH'). So, it's totally possible that Helel or Lucifer, whatever you want to call him, was chief over 1/3 of the angels whose job was praising the most High. This would make some sense when you think about how evil and powerful most secular music is (and even some "worship" music) and how Satan has used all entertainment, especially music, to control people and direct the praise of the people back to himself. In this way he receives worship from those made in the image of the most High. There is also debate as to whether Satan was a cherub or a seraph. The Seraphim are considered by theologians to be the most powerful, and actually in the form of serpents or dragons, and guarding the throne of God. When I first heard that I was really surprised. We spend so much time looking at snakes as evil, that I was surprised to know that the most powerful angels who guard the throne of God are actually serpents. So, it's natural for people to want to say Satan was a seraph, since we see him in the form of a serpent in the garden. It's completely possible that at one time he was a full dragon with legs and wings, and then his legs and wings were removed as a punishment for deceiving Eve. But we also see in Ezekiel 28: 11-19, it appears that Satan is called both the anointed cherub and the covering cherub. People argue this isn't the case since the King of Tyre is addressed, but it also says he was there in the Garden of Eden, so he couldn't have just been a regular man. People have a really hard time understanding how in the Bible sometimes two things are true simultaneously. This whole conversation is interesting but the debate is really beyond the scope of this book. I understand that there is a hierarchy of authority in heaven, and that there are some angels with more authority than others. The more time you spend researching what other people believe about all of these entities, the more confused you are likely to become. There are endless debates online about the different classes of angels, and how to interpret the information we find in scripture about them. You'll always find some in the debates who bring in "extra-biblical" sources. I'm not going to speak against or for these other sources. I haven't studied them enough yet to confirm or refute people's trust in them. The book of Enoch (Enoch 1 was actually found along with the manuscripts in the dead sea scrolls) and the Apocrypha (group of 14 or so books that are widely rejected by the Protestant Church, and accepted by the Roman Catholic Church) are two of the more common extra-biblical texts people draw from, and there are tons of other writings from men going back hundreds of years that people like to point to. I'm less concerned with all of this. I know angels exist. I have two direct experiences where I know I interacted with an angel that I will share in the I Am Spiritual chapter. I think it's cool to consider an entire group of creation that we don't know very well, but will one day join in worshipping our King. It is helpful to understand that these entities exist when trying to make sense of everything, and especially when engaging in spiritual warfare. We will go through all of that later. But since Satan is a fallen angel, and we're in the chapter exposing our enemy, we had to introduce angels here. It doesn't really matter to us right now when you get down to it; no matter what his exact original created appearance was, we know several things about him. He was considered beautiful. He is very wise and crafty. We know that he masquerades as an angel of light and is able to change his appearance. We know he was eventually jealous of God and rebelled. He was able to convince a third of the angels to rebel with him, and a war was fought (which they lost). We know he can enter inside people (Luke 22:3 Satan entered Judas). We know that he is responsible for the fallen state of mankind by deceiving Eve into eating from the forbidden tree. We know that he wanders to and fro on earth now, and has to go before the throne of God to petition who he can attack. We know that he commands an army of demons that are here on earth (demons are not fallen-angels but we will cover that shortly). We know that he cometh not but for to steal, kill, and destroy. We know that he has already caused the entire world to be destroyed before. We know that he plans to execute the saints of the most High, and that he is preparing to go to war with Jesus when He returns. We know that he plans to one day sit on the throne of God. We know that we look like God, and that Satan does not. We also know from 1 Corinthians 6:3 that we will one day judge/ govern the angels. There is much that we may never know about angels, demons, and our great enemy. But we know enough that we can identify when he is attacking us, and we know enough that we can be victorious over him. We know that if we are obedient to God and resist Satan, he will flee from us.

Submit yourselves therefore to God. Resist the devil, and he will flee from you.

James 4:7

These two conditions above must be met if we hope to be victorious against this very powerful enemy. First, we must submit ourselves to God. This is done by accepting that He is LORD, by choosing to accept Jesus as His son and the only propitiation for your sins. It means truly repenting of any and all of your sins, and committing yourself to trying your best to avoid sin in the future. It also means listening to His Holy Spirit, and generally being obedient to any action He calls you to. If you are not in submission (fully surrendered) to God, then He won't (usually) give you authority to defeat Satan in battle. IF you are in submission to God, THEN you are a servant He will anoint with His power to overcome the devil more consistently. But you still have to resist the devil. Again, with the rottweiler and chihuahua. Just because you are anointed and it's God's power not yours, does not mean that you don't have a role to play. A US Naval Admiral does not personally own a Navy fleet, but is given authority to command it. What would happen though if he just read a book or took a nap instead of giving commands? The authority would not be exercised, and the weapons would be as good as useless if they're not being used *(obviously I understand others would step up in his absence, I was just using the analogy of a person who is delegated authority over a very powerful set of weapons to prove the point that you have an active role to play)*. We're going to take a look at many of the tactics of our terrible enemy, but unless you are submitting to God and actively resisting the devil, it would be uselessly dormant information. Let's take a look at the devil's tactics, so we can create a plan of attack.

Now the serpent was more subtil than any beast of the field which the LORD God had made. And he said unto the woman, Yea, hath God said, Ye shall not eat of every tree of the garden? And the woman said unto the serpent, We may eat of the fruit of the trees of the garden: But of the fruit of the tree which is in the midst of the garden, God hath said, Ye shall not eat of it, neither shall ye touch it, lest ye die. And the serpent said unto the woman, Ye shall not surely die: For God doth know that in the day ye eat thereof, then your eyes shall be opened, and ye shall be as gods, knowing good and evil.

Genesis 3:1-5

The word "subtil" here means crafty, shrewd, and sly. If you think about it, he has to be. A snake isn't the fasted or strongest animal; it's pretty weak in the order of things really. It's only able to completely consume small prey like rats or vulnerable little birds' eggs (children are a delicacy he apparently prefers). So, he has to be subtil. He has to try to trick people. How does he do this? He "said unto the woman". Remember our whole chapter on language? He spoke words that were not technically fully completely true, but these words still had power in them. Sometimes he lies outright. Usually, he wraps his lies with some bits of truth. Like in this case with Eve; she didn't die immediately upon eating the forbidden fruit, but she did eventually die, so he was still a liar. But, since Eve didn't immediately die, Adam was also persuaded to give in to the temptation. It looked like the serpent had told them the truth, and that the fruit was good for them. It looked, for a moment, like maybe God was just withholding something good and desirable from them. But then, like always happens with sin, eventually the full truth came out, they regretted their decision, and felt shame. This is Satan's modus operandi. He did it with the angels before Eve. He, through his words, was able to persuade them that there was more that was good or desirable to them that God was withholding from them. He promised them that the grass was greener somewhere in a different field under a different shepherd. They believed his lies long enough to act, and then suffered the consequences. In addition to the lies he tells us to tempt us, he also sells us the lie that we can be like God.

We see these two attacks play out over and over again in life:

1. Satan carefully crafts some lie, hides a deception inside some half-truth, and
2. Convinces people to reject the word and authority of God Almighty in an attempt to avoid being dominated, and to be "like/as" God ourselves.

All of his other attacks are basically just variations of this strategy.

His talents (the ability to remain invisible to the physical eye, and the ability to deceive with lies) are how he stays in the game. God chooses to remain hidden so we are not destroyed by the power of His glory, and so our free will can exist in choosing Him or rejecting Him, allowing true love to exist. Satan hides because he is a liar, a coward, and a thief. Staying hidden is the only chance he has to gain power over us. If he revealed himself to us, most people would resist him. As we saw in my testimony of the time he revealed himself to me, if he (Satan) exists, then we know He (God Almighty) exists too, right? So, it behooves Satan and his agenda to remain hidden so we don't resist him, and it behooves him to remain hidden so we don't focus on the reality that there is a sovereign God who loves us and blesses us, but who also has standards and a set of rules to which He expects us to adhere. In this way, Satan wins small victories, and even if he doesn't really think he is going to win the final war, he will spitefully take down any of God's children that he can, before he is thrown into the lake of fire. This is really the only way Satan can hurt God. He knows that God loves those made in His image, so if Satan can hurt us, or cause any of us to be separated from God, he knows how much this will grieve God. Satan is a spiteful, prideful little brat that would rather destroy something good than allow someone else to enjoy it.

Some people, through their use of sorcery/ pharmakeia (drug use), or through other occultic practices "force" the veil open so they are able to see into the spiritual realm. I already mentioned that this opens them up to deceiving spirits. God allows this "forcing" of the veil so that people reap what they are sowing from their rebellion, disobedience, and wickedness. When someone crosses into this part of the spiritual realm, Satan, other fallen angels, and demons are able to manifest to the person where the person can see them. Most often though, if they think they have a chance at deceiving the person, they change their appearance so that they appear as something they know the person will like. We will go into more on all of this in the I Am Spiritual chapter, but this is why so many in the New Age cult are deceived. They think they are seeing some beautiful spiritual entity that wants to help them (i.e., a spirit guide), but in reality, these spirits are just in a spiritual costume of sorts, which they use to lure the fool deeper and further into chaos.

And no marvel; for Satan himself is transformed into an angel of light.

2 Corinthians 11:14

We've talked a little about how Satan is a person without a body, therefore invisible to our physical eyes, and how this is one of his major advantages in his war against humanity. Let's take a look now at his other great strength. How is he so crafty and able to deceive everyone so masterfully with his words?

The Serpent's Bifurcated Tongue

In nature, the serpents bifurcated tongue flicks about, gathering chemicals from the environment around it, and bringing them to the roof of its mouth where the information can be processed as smells. God could have created the snake in such a way that this function could have been performed without the tongue being split/ bifurcated. I understand scientifically the benefit of the bifurcation to the snake in terms of giving it better location information, but I believe God also chose to design the snake with two parts to its tongue to teach us something about the spiritual nature of our enemy. Literally every time he speaks, there is dual meaning.

In scripture we are commanded to let our "yes" be "yes" and our "no" be "no". There's a reason that lying is listing among the sins-unto-death. Speaking words that are not true creates disorder, chaos, and death. Speaking words that are true creates order and life. Every time God speaks, it is 100% truth and therefore life. Every time Satan speaks, there is poison and death hidden underneath a morsel of truth. He will never speak plainly, or without ulterior motive. The only reason this tactic is successful is because people are ignorant to the truth of some matters, and he exploits this weakness. Here is one example:

You've heard the expression, "ignorance is bliss" right? To a small degree this can be somewhat true, in that if you are ignorant to something that would trouble you, there is a season of time where that reality is not in your awareness, so you don't have to deal with it yet. What's true though, is the temporary vacation from reality usually costs you more later, since it was not addressed sooner. A leak in your boat is a decent example. So, while Satan says "ignorance is bliss" God tells us in Hosea 4:6 ~

My people are destroyed for lack of knowledge

Not only does this show us an example of one of Satan's half-truth's, it also speaks to the importance of working with true information. If someone knows the truth about a topic, they are much less likely to fall victim to believing a lie. I'll give you another example from the gym. We had a member there who came from a military family. Both his father and his older brother were highly decorated, but he (the younger brother) never served. I guess he heard lots of stories around the dinner table, and felt like he didn't measure up or something. This guy showed up to the gym and created this whole persona that he was an Army Ranger and had all these stories about his military service. Many of the members including myself somewhat bought into the possibility that he was telling the truth. He seemed a little off, but kind, and claimed he suffered from PTSD so I gave him the benefit of the doubt. Since I never served in the armed forces, I didn't know the right questions to ask to qualify his claims. I even gave the guy a military discount on his membership. But it didn't take long before he encountered a genuine American hero working out. One of our members was a veteran who served in Iraq and saw lots of combat. It took maybe one minute total before the real veteran identified with clarity the attempt at stolen valor, and the entire charade was quickly over. It would be like this for us in life, when Satan tries to lie to us, if we knew the truth about whatever situation we faced. When we have real experience in an area, we are less vulnerable in that area. This is why children are targeted. They know very little, and are gullible and impressionable. Satan knows the best time to plant seeds in a person's life is while they are young, and his attack on people begins while they are still in the womb. This is why the book of Proverbs goes to great length describing the importance of wisdom, and how wisdom will help you to avoid terrible suffering. We will discuss further in the I Am Intellectual chapter some helpful ways to fill yourself with, access, and harness wisdom. But, for now, back to the loser/ enemy we all have to deal with…

Not only do we have to face the issue of discerning the words we hear from our adversary, but since he is invisible, the fight is even more unfair, because with him being invisible and speaking in the spirit,

WE OFTEN HEAR HIS VOICE AS OUR OWN.

He has studied us, like an actor would study the person they are playing in a movie, and knows how to mimic us closely. Then, when he thinks the moment is right, he whispers in our ear some thought. We then have a choice to make. We either accept the voice and agree with it, or we reject it. This might look something like this:

"I should just copy the answer on the person's paper next to me. They'll never know and it doesn't really hurt anything"

In that moment you have a choice to make and normally you will follow up with some words, whether audibly or even just inside your head. You either say, *"Yeah it won't matter"* and go ahead and cheat, or you say, *"No, I'm not going to cheat, I'll just do my best on my own"*.

Most people process the conversation I just wrote as if the entire conversation was their own. Maybe it was. Our own flesh is wicked enough that we can't pass all of the blame off on the devil and give him too much credit. But, it's also possible that another spirit was present and speaking.

The enemy starts tempting us early in life, and he always begins with small, seemingly insignificant temptations. Like the cheating on the test example above. Still technically wrong, but it's not like you killed someone right? Most people recognize the really big sins from far off, and cannot even begin to consider that they would do such a thing. It's true that people who suffer horrible abuse sometimes get a head start down the road of destruction and become capable of doing great harm to others, but we also see instances where there wasn't any childhood trauma and a person still becomes a liar, a thief, a murderer, etc. How is this? Satan knows people really well. He understands what level of temptation will be a true temptation for you. If he whispered something abhorrent to you, you wouldn't do it, but if he starts with something you do really want that is only slightly outside of your moral "fence", then he knows if he can get you to look at it enough, eventually you are going to open the gate and reach outside. He puts it really close to the gate to start, so you feel safe and think nobody will see or find out, and think there won't be any consequences. And then, when you think you have gotten away with it, he places the candy an inch further away from the gate. Eventually he trains you to just leave the gate open, and you effectively end up with no fence. This is how secret societies work too (wonder where they learned it?). They start out promising you that you will be blessed, and help others. You take some really "small" oath and get some sweet rewards. Then eventually you need to give some more, and make a deeper commitment, but the reward structure still seems like it's worth it. Eventually in order to level up, you have to do something they can blackmail you with, "so you can be trusted" with the deeper secrets and greater power. Eventually you are doing terrible things on your own, and you may have even been conditioned to believe you actually like it. But they don't start there; they start with some "innocent" fun at a frat party. Satan follows this procedure over and over again. If you resist a temptation, he says, "ok we need to dial it back a little", and he starts over.

The Temptation Machine

A big contributor to why most Christians never go deeper in their faith, is not the major, super-terrible, clearly abhorrent sins, but the "small" ones that they never seem to overcome. Most people don't start out leaning into gross darkness; they simply excuse the decision to embrace what they want to believe is a "gray area", or some "small" compromise in their morals or integrity. Ten small steps still cover the same distance as one giant leap. This is how your enemy eventually lures most people miles away from righteousness into perversion, lawlessness, disobedience, idolatry, and the eventual hardening of one's heart with the outright acceptance, celebration, and worship of that which is evil.

There is a cycle, therefore, that is always being perpetuated:

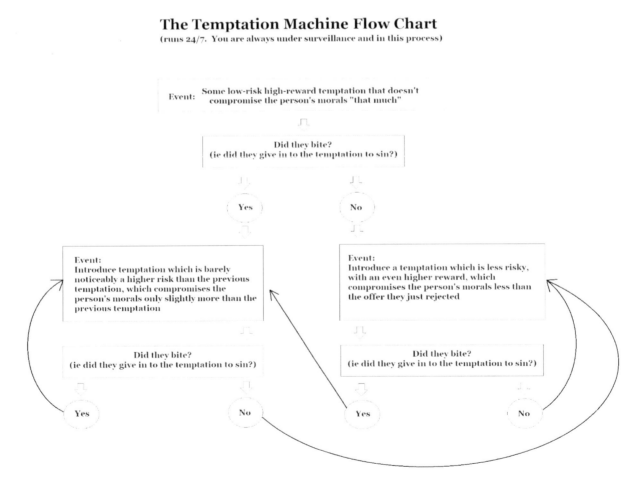

The Temptation Machine Flow Chart
(runs 24/7. You are always under surveillance and in this process)

This temptation machine is always running, but when you say "no", the machine slows down. When you say "yes", the machine speeds up. We will talk later in multiple places about the importance of exercising your "no" muscle. The significance of this really can't be overstated. You have to win the small battles. They will normally ALL seem small to you, because in your flesh, your bar for what is morally right shifts as your heart hardens. Most people don't even realize it happening. This is why we cannot rely on ourselves to decide what is morally acceptable. This is why the Lord, in His brilliance, made a standard for us to follow and wrote it down for us in His Word. That way, no matter where we have allowed this temptation machine to take us, we can always check ourselves against the standard and see if we need to say "no" to some things that we currently don't have a personal moral conviction against. Maybe we need to level down some to bring our bar back in line with God's? With this machine, Satan is happy to win <u>any</u> level of your yes-to-temptation. He plays the long game, and will move you one micrometer at a time, if that is all you are willing to give him. He will gladly take any victory, no matter how small. We have to study God's Word to understand where the boundaries and standards are, and then hold ourselves to them. We have to choose to take this on personally. That way, we will be victorious in shutting down the temptation machine that our flesh creates for us, and the temptation machine that Satan runs us through. We create enough of our own problems with our sinful lustful flesh. And then we also give place to Satan and these demonic spirits that try to mimic our voice in our head spiritually. Satan, (and his demons) participate in this infiltration campaign constantly. Most Christians ignorantly give Satan way too much credit. Any time something bad happens they say the devil did it. In one sense they are right, since he is the father of lies, the prince of darkness, and the temporary god of this world. But one of the ways that Satan wants to be like the most High is that he wants to be omni-present, because he IS NOT. God Almighty/ the Holy Spirit can simultaneously speak to every single person on earth at the exact same time and carry-on individual conversations with all of us. Satan cannot. God is everywhere at the same time. Satan is limited to time and space. He has to be in one location at a time. The way that he still has influence over the whole earth is through his subordinates, the demons.

Demons are not fallen angels; they are distinct and separate from each other. The exact origin of demons is not given in the canon of scripture, but the prevailing theory is that demons are the disembodied spirits of the Nephilim. The Nephilim were the offspring produced when the fallen angels came down, took the daughters of men, saw that they were beautiful, and had intercourse with them. This is all detailed in Genesis 6. We will talk more about the giants that ruled the earth in later chapters. But for now, we will just introduce that the reason God flooded the earth was not just because the hearts of men had become wicked. It was because ALL FLESH HAD BECOME CORRUPTED. There is nothing new under the sun. All of this gene manipulation we see today is not new science. The fallen angels came down, created a hybrid race of beings, and then started mixing humans with animals. It got to the point that Noah and his sons were the only genetically pure humans left on earth. This is why it says in Genesis 6:9 that Noah was "perfect in his generations". He wasn't spared because he was perfectly holy. We see him getting drunk right after the flood dried up, so it wasn't just his behavior that saved him. He was perfect in his DNA. The most likely source of all the demonic activity in the world today is that when God flooded the earth, all of the millions and potentially billions of living creatures on the dry earth died, but their spirits stayed here on earth rather than being sent to hell. Now, these spirits wander around the earth, dehydrated and looking for homes (bodies) in which to dwell. Sometimes (often) they find a suitable host with an open doorway and make themselves comfortable inside, setting up residence. But even those whose hedge of protection has not been broken can still hear them whispering and yelling from outside. We will go through all of this in greater detail when we talk about deliverance and spiritual warfare in the I Am Spiritual chapter, but for now just know that Satan and his demons speak *to* people and *through* people. This is how the kingdom of Satan has been built, is maintained, and advances. Though his network is vast, and his influence great, Satan still knows that he is weak sauce compared to the King of Kings. He has been working to build a kingdom that relies less on his imperfect employees to get the job done (anyone who has owned a business or managed people knows how hard it can be to find decent help). Satan is working to build a physical network where he can mimic the most High and manage the whole world himself through the use of technology, rather than depending mostly on his cronies. We will break down Satan's strategy for dominating the entire world and mimicking the most High in greater detail in The End of the Age/ End Time Prophecy Analysis chapter. But for now, we are still just laying the groundwork to understand the current battle we are in on a day-to-day basis.

Satan's double speak is reproduced when people repeat what they hear him say. In this way he has been able to manipulate society and spread an anti-Christ spirit throughout cultures worldwide. Most of the hard-core leftist/ communist ideology has some glimmer or pretense of righteousness to it. The ideals are simply not founded in truth or wisdom unfortunately, and break down when applied in the real world. It's a nice idea, for example, to give everyone a universal basic income and "free" healthcare. Who doesn't want their basic necessities taken care of? But the nice idea breaks down when implementation is attempted, because in this physical world manual effort is required to produce products and offer services. So, a person is either compensated for their efforts to serve someone by sacrificing their time and energy, or they are effectively enslaved. Human beings require food, water, and shelter and these needs require work to produce. It's the curse from the garden that has never left us. When Adam sinned, the LORD cursed him to work by the sweat of his brow, and that he would toil all the days of his life. This is painful and people still don't want to accept it. This reality is present, whether we want to admit it or not, and when people listen to the lie that a different reality is possible, chaos is sown and eventually produces chaotic, destructive fruit. Satan does not stop weaving his crafty little lies throughout culture, and carefully inching the world one step closer to chaos and destruction, daily. Our poor world and the people here are so deeply entangled in a web of confusion that we are past the point of no return. It's a valiant effort, of course, to stand for truth and to do our best to push back against all of the madness. I'm doing my best to do exactly that with the writing of this book. But we know based on Bible prophesy that we're not going to be able to reverse the damage. The Lord is simply allowing the wheat and the tares to grow up together. Eventually, He will sort them and clean up this mess. Our efforts to push back against foolish, evil lies is with the hopes that we will be able to snatch a soul or two out from Satan's grasp, and to break the chains of demonic oppression off of them. We have to at least try to pull people out of the fire, or there will be blood on our hands.

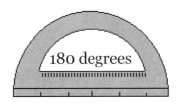

The goal of the serpent's lying tongue, is that as much as possible, he wants to pervert the minds of people as far from truth as possible. In many cases, he has been successful in confusing people to believe something that is the complete opposite of the truth. As we see on a protractor, his goal is to get you 180 degrees away from the truth (remember that chaos is 180 degrees away from order on our Order vs Chaos line). Sadly, he is often successful at this. We will expose many of these gross lies as we go through this I Am Well series. But keep in mind, as my brother Derek Prince stated, ~ "any degree of variation from the truth is still crooked, it matters not if it is only one degree, the reality is, it is still crooked" *(not an exact quote of his, but I remember him saying something very close to this in a teaching)*. Just like Satan is happy to move you one micrometer at a time with the temptation machine, a similar process is underway where he is trying to get you to accept and believe lies. If he can get you to believe a 180 degree lie, then he has hit a homerun, but he will accept any level of your agreement to/ acceptance of a lie, even if that lie is only 1 degree off from the truth. In the same way that he slowly inches us further away from God's standard of morality with the temptation machine, he also slowly inches our entire world away from believing truth into believing lies, one little 1 degree lie at a time until the foundations of our understanding are destroyed, and we are easily tossed to and fro. Our only hope to find the real-deal truth in this corrupted world is to turn to Jesus. Only He can give us the spiritual eyes to see through all of the lies and deceptions that the world at large, and even well-meaning Christians, have been taught to perpetuate through their ignorant regurgitation. A few more pertinent verses come to mind:

And the great dragon was cast out, that old serpent, called the Devil, and Satan, which deceiveth the whole world: he was cast out into the earth, and his angels were cast out with him.

Revelation 12:9

For there shall arise false Christs, and false prophets, and shall shew great signs and wonders; insomuch that, if it were possible, they shall deceive the very elect.

Matthew 24:24

And then shall that Wicked be revealed, whom the Lord shall consume with the spirit of his mouth, and shall destroy with the brightness of his coming: Even him, whose coming is after the working of Satan with all power and signs and lying wonders, And with all deceivableness of unrighteousness in them that perish; because they received not the love of the truth, that they might be saved. And for this cause God shall send them strong delusion, that they should believe a lie: That they all might be damned who believed not the truth, but had pleasure in unrighteousness.

2 Thessalonians 2:8-12

That we henceforth be no more children, tossed to and fro, and carried about with every wind of doctrine, by the sleight of men, and cunning craftiness, whereby they lie in wait to deceive; But speaking the truth in love, may grow up into him in all things, which is the head, even Christ: From whom the whole body fitly joined together and compacted by that which every joint supplieth, according to the effectual working in the measure of every part, maketh increase of the body unto the edifying of itself in love. This I say therefore, and testify in the Lord, that ye henceforth walk not as other Gentiles walk, in the vanity of their mind, Having the understanding darkened, being alienated from the life of God through the ignorance that is in them, because of the blindness of their heart: Who being past feeling have given themselves over unto lasciviousness, to work all uncleanness with greediness. But ye have not so learned Christ; If so be that ye have heard him, and have been taught by him, as the truth is in Jesus: That ye put off concerning the former conversation the old man, which is corrupt according to the deceitful lusts; And be renewed in the spirit of your mind; And that ye put on the new man, which after God is created in righteousness and true holiness. Wherefore putting away lying, speak every man truth with his neighbour: for we are members one of another.

Ephesians 4:14-25

If the foundations be destroyed, what can the righteous do?

Psalm 11:3

The last tactic I want to very briefly expose for now is Satan's attack on male leadership. Satan understands God's design for spiritual authority much better than do we. He understands that God has given man authority over his wife, his home, his children, and over spiritual entities. This makes man Satan's 1st priority target. Satan knows that if he can take out the man, everyone who is under that man's authority will suffer. He knows that the only hope he has of winning any battles with his wimpy little cohort, is if he can distract a man from exercising his spiritual authority against the kingdom of darkness. I know at this point there are probably some of you who are feeling a certain kind of way about hearing that it is the man who has the highest authority under God. Likely this is because you were under a man at some point (or perhaps repeatedly) who failed to exercise his authority with integrity, and you suffered to some degree from this failure. Likely, the man who let you down in your life did not love his wife and serve his family "as Christ loved the church and gave himself up for her". Ephesians 5:25 shows that a man is supposed to be willing to sacrifice everything for the benefit of his bride. A woman who has truly been loved by a man who is willing to suffer for her like Christ suffered on the cross, does not have a problem submitting to his leadership. She can rest assured, knowing that no matter what comes, the man's heart is in the right place and that he is submitting to God, therefore his leadership will most often be correct. We will break down more on this dynamic later, but for now we are just introducing in our chapter on The Enemy, why he targets men. We will break down some of the "how" he targets men as we go along. But for now, let this be a call for all men who are reading this to rise to the call of leadership. Rise to the call to serve your family. Rise to the call to protect them. Rise to the call to give yourself up for them. Women, rise to the call to love and respect your husbands. Pray for them as often as you can, and pray not only that they would be men that you could submit to, but pray also that you would indeed submit to them in earnest humility. This is not to say that women aren't called to fight or have authority. Of course they are and of course they do! The first judge, Deborah, was a woman for example, and a mighty warrior. But the reality is, men were created to be the head. Most of the time we see women stepping up valiantly to lead today, it's the byproduct of a male leadership void, resulting from Satan's attack on men. In many of these situations, the family, and ultimately the entire community, suffers from the mother not fulfilling her unique role, because she is busy doing the job that the men were too lazy, too weak, or too selfish to do. Like I said, we will cover more on this tactic as we go through this series. But for now, just be aware that the destruction of the man and his authority, is one of Satan's highest priorities. He devotes a massive amount of energy toward this end. The esteemed pastor, writer, and leadership champion Dr. John Maxwell is quoted as saying, "Everything rises and falls on leadership". He is

128

wise and correct. I would take it a step further though and say, "Everything rises and falls on *male* leadership". I will do my best throughout the remainder of this I Am Well series to call men to leadership, and to explain why this is so critical in our wellness battle.

Satan's tactics are so extensive that it would be impractical to try to go into great detail on all of them here, but as we work through each remaining chapter in the series, I will try to expose the ones you are likely to encounter as they become relevant in each wellness component's conversation. Just know that the kingdom of darkness is a tightly organized military unit, and the entities within Satan's organization are governed by principalities. As criminal as they are, they MUST obey true authority when true authority has been delegated and is exercised. As we work our way through the remainder of this series, I will help you to recognize many of Satan's tactics, tools, and agents. You will begin to see, taste, hear, feel and smell right through the temptations, fear, false religions, lies, controlled oppositions, dishonest semantics, and general shenaniganry of the lord of dung. You will be able to recognize his handiwork in your life, and in the lives of others. You will take back any power you have given him and his goons. You will start to win mighty victories and claim territory for the kingdom of God. I'll help you to pour into each of your wellness cups, and to punch the dragon in his face when he tries to stop you. I'll help you to gain the courage, confidence, and faith to know that through obedience to Jesus, you too will crush the head of the serpent.

I know there have been many times so far that I have spoken in an insulting, demeaning way about our terrible enemy. Do not mistake this for a second to mean that I don't respect him. I actually have a great level of respect for the power he controls, his intelligence, his talent, his beauty, his team, and the damage he could do to me and my family if God removed His hand of protection from my life. Like Pastor Marcus Rogers always says, "Casual Christians will be casualties". So, as you become empowered to fight back against the kingdom of darkness, don't become arrogant. The Archangel Michael didn't even do that. In Jude 1:9 in contending with the devil, his humble response was, "the Lord rebuke thee". I turned my back on a group of high-level freemasons and satanist witches (who I knew were actively gathered and joined together in cursing me) once, and I suffered for it. I'll tell you more later, but I couldn't stand for two weeks, and it took me months of rehab to miraculously recover from what could have been a crippling injury. This is no game. This is no joke. We're playing for keeps and the stakes are the highest possible. So, avoid the errors on either side of this road. We have a terrible enemy. Don't give him too much credit, but also don't take the battle too lightly. You must commit your full energy toward vigilance, you must submit to God and choose faith, and you must choose to fight multiple battles at once with all the strength God gives you. It's not going to be an easy victory. But the victory will be, and it will be glorious. I'd like to wrap up this chapter with a quick preview of end time prophesy, to show you what is the future fate of our enemy when this is all over, and the dust has settled.

And the devil that deceived them was cast into the lake of fire and brimstone, where the beast and the false prophet are, and shall be tormented day and night for ever and ever.

Revelation 20:10

HalleluYah!

Selah

Suggested Closing Prayer for Non-Christians: The Enemy

(Recommended to be spoken out loud)

Wow. God, if you are real and any of this talk about the devil is real, I want to know the truth. If you are real and you really do love me, please show me. If the devil is real and actively trying to kill me, please show me and please protect me. If demons are attacking me, please show me and please help me. If my heart is hardened toward you and that's blocking me from seeing your hand working in my life and keeping me from hearing your voice, please soften my heart so I can see you and hear you. If you are real, please help me to know that, and help me to seek after you. If heaven and hell are real, please don't let me send myself to hell. If heaven is real, I want to go there when I die. Please send your Holy Spirit to help me find the one true path to you through your son Jesus. Please don't let me be destroyed in my ignorance. Please help me to find victory.

In Jesus' name, Amen

Suggested Closing Prayer for Christians: The Enemy

(Recommended to be spoken out loud)

Heavenly Father, thank you so much for this day, and for the luxury of the time to read and study. Thank you for your protection and provision. If anything Jonathan wrote about our enemy is incorrect or incomplete, please correct our understanding. If I am resistant to accepting anything that Jonathan wrote as true, if it really is true, I pray you soften my heart, reduce my pride, and help me to receive any truth that really is from you. Help me to understand just how active Satan and his demons are in my life. Please show me anywhere that I have broken your hedge of protection around my life, and help me to correct whatever is wrong in my heart. Father, please help me to resist the temptation to sin. Please help me to be courageous and selfless in this fight. Please help me to find the time and energy to continue reading and studying this I Am Well series. Please help Jonathan to finish this assignment with integrity and excellence. Please help us to defeat the enemy. Please continue to help us be well.

In Jesus' name, Amen